LogoPower®

*creating world-class logos
and effective identities*

> Includes a CD-Rom to help you prepare a
> corporate graphic standards manual
> for your company or clients.

David E. Carter

Illustrations by
Jenette D'Tallè

Book Designer
Suzanna M.W. Brown

The Carter Library of Design

**LogoPower — Creating world-class logos
and effective identities.**

LogoPower® is a registered trademark of
Decathlon Corporation,
a division of David E. Carter, Inc.

First published 1998 by Hearst Books International
1350 Avenue of the Americas
New York, NY 10019

ISBN: 0688-16042-5

Distributed in the U.S. and Canada by
Watson-Guptill Publications
1515 Broadway
New York, NY 10036
Tel: (800) 451-1741
             (908) 363-4511 in NJ, AK, HI
Fax: (908) 363-0338

Distributed throughout the rest of the world by
Hearst Books International
1350 Avenue of the Americas
New York, NY 10019
Fax: (212) 261-6795

ISBN: 0-8230-6603-7

Printed in Hong Kong by Everbest Printing Company
through Four Colour Imports, Louisville, Kentucky.

LogoPower®
table of contents

At last, the Ultimate Book
on Corporate Identity Manuals

In 1976, I produced a book called **Corporate Identity Manuals**. It was the first of its kind: a very thick book (nearly 500 pages) which included 13 complete corporate identity manuals from a variety of companies.

For the first time, thousands of designers got to look at a cross-section of quality identity systems. A couple of the manuals (Pitney Bowes and Sherwin Williams) gave insight into how large firms can control the uses of their logos to assure consistent usage.

In that book, I wrote:

> **A weak symbol, applied consistently is more effective than a better symbol which is not used uniformly.**

That is the basic premise behind having a corporate identity manual. Every firm needs to present the best image possible…and the manual is the one way to assure consistent usage of the logo.

The 1976 book was highly successful. At the time, it was very expensive—$30. Still, it sold several thousand copies and had four printings.

But the book did more than just sell. It allowed colleges and art schools to offer courses in corporate identity. Literally thousands of students over the years have used **Corporate Identity Manuals** as part of their design education.

For a number of years, I have received frequent calls from art educators who ask, "When are you going to update **Corporate Identity Manuals**?"

For a long time, I didn't have an answer. Until now.

I've been planning this book for several years, but most of the time was spent just deciding how to do it.

So — here's how we decided to do it:

- The book would unfold as a single project—as a huge project for a mythical corporation.

- The book would begin with a design project: create a new logo for a company. This section of the book would take the reader through the "real life" steps that are typical of a major design job.

- Then, once the logo had been approved, a very detailed set of graphic standards—call it the Ultimate Corporate Identity Manual — would be produced.

- And to make this book highly useful for experienced designers as well as students, we would include notes on the project wherever we felt it would be helpful.

- Finally, we decided to include a CD-ROM with all the identity templates shown in this book — more than 300. They're in EPS format for both Macintosh and PC users on the CD that comes with this publication. That alone should be well worth the price of this book.

So, here it is. If readers find this book as useful as the original book, we will have done our job.

David E. Carter

The Mythical Corporation:
some background

Since this book focuses on a mythical corporate identity project for a business that we're calling The Mythical Corporation, we begin with some information business. (All successful corporate identity projects begin with a thorough study of the company's past, as well as its goals.)

The Mythical Corporation was once a highly successful passenger railroad business. Like most other passenger rail lines, they lost share of market to the airlines, personal cars, bicycles, walking, and just about any other means of getting from one place to another.

But in its heyday, The Mythical Corporation was a well-run railroad. Its logo, shown below, left no doubt as to the central business of the firm.

As changes took place in The Mythical Corporation's competitive arena, much of its services became obsolete. People stopped traveling by rail, and the company's freight business generated only a small portion of the revenue that its once lucrative passenger market provided.

As Mythical management tried to think of creative solutions to this change of market preference, the firm had a major asset that was not being utilized: it had literally thousands of miles of rail tracks sitting unused on narrow ribbons of land which it owned. It had a number of now abandoned passenger terminals in major cities.

While the value of Mythical stock was on a slow

descent, a couple of things happened to change the company's future.

- Congress passed a national "let's ride bikes more" law, which encouraged unused rail routes to be converted into bicycle-only roads.

- The changing urban demographics suddenly caused several of the Mythical train stations to become prime real estate, each of them worth millions to developers of downtown properties.

Suddenly, The Mythical Corporation became flush with cash. New management was brought in to take advantage of the opportunity to invest in expanded areas of business and industry.

In a several month period, Mythical acquired a number of diverse businesses, and changed from a dying rail business into a conglomerate.

Now, Mythical has a corporate identity problem. Its old logo is still in use. The company is no longer just a railroad. It now owns diverse divisions such as an airline, hotel, car rental, banks…etc.

Why would The Mythical Corporation diversify into so many areas? 1. Cash does strange things to people, and 2. This book requires a very broad base of businesses in order to show the Ultimate Identity Manual.

So—from this point forward, you're in the world of The Mythical Corporation. You'll see each step of how their new logo is created, and you'll watch as the corporate identity manual is put together.

In the process, you should learn a great deal about the process of logo creation, as well as how (and why) to create a highly-detailed corporate identity manual.

Aaaaaacme Designs'
roughs_____

The Mythical CEO realized that the firm had out-grown its old logo. He went to the yellow pages, called Aaaaaacme Logo Designs, and said "I want a new logo for The Mythical Corporation." The designer, lacking much experience, immediately went to work without asking any questions (except "will the check clear?").

Two days later, the designer presented these roughs.

This is **NOT** the way to begin a logo design project.
The next few pages will show the right way to
undertake corporate identity design.

Notes on
trademark law

When the Mythical CEO saw a couple of the logos presented by the designer from Aaaaaacme, he thought they looked a little familiar. Then he remembered some horror stories about a big company coming up with a logo that already belonged to someone else.

Fearful of making a big (*footnote*, see expensive) mistake, he called James R. Higgins, Jr., an attorney who practices considerable trademark law, and asked for some guidelines. Here's what he learned from Mr. Higgins:

General Legal Comments

1. The legal mission of a trademark is to "identify and distinguish" one company's goods and services from those offered by competitors. Thus, the goal in selecting a trademark or service mark is to choose a mark that is legally "distinctive."

Use fanciful type or a "secondary device" to add distinctiveness. (Caveat: if the name is nondistinctive, adding fanciful type or a secondary device will only create protection for the name containing those distinctive elements; e.g., the only thing protectable about **Ǎcme** is the use of the **Ǎ** and the script **cme**. The common company name "Acme" could be used by others without infringing rights in the fancy **Ǎcme**.) That's why it is a good idea, when possible, to use arbitrary nondescriptive words as the base portion of the mark.

Ǎcme

2. A significant benefit to using a "secondary device" is that it provides a unifying identifier for a range of products or services from your company. For example, computer consumers have come to know, and rely on, (and, especially, buy from) Compaq, the company with the distinctive "Q." A proper secondary device, like McDonald's "Golden Arches" or the Nike "swoosh" or the Spalding Top Flite "fancy F", can become a symbol which provides instant distinctiveness and consumer recognition.

3. Do not be naive in thinking that just because you "independently" selected a secondary device, this will avoid all problems. In trademark law, a secondary device is a design, searchable just like the base words of a mark. It would still be an infringement if, for example, Acme Bank decided to use the Nike "swoosh" as a secondary device. It could be just as much an infringement if you choose a design already being used by a smaller company who didn't do business in your area. (When the senior user entered your area, you'd have to stop.)

Information on the legal aspects of logo design was supplied by James R. Higgins, Jr., an attorney who practices considerable trade mark law. Contact: James R. Higgins, Jr. Middleton & Reutlinger, 2500 Brown & Williamson Tower, Louisville, KY 40202 (502) 584-1135.

The larger the firm, the greater the danger

In general, companies with large areas of trade (such as regional, national, or multinational) have to exercise greater care in choosing a trademark. A principle of trademark law is to allow two innocent entities to use the same trademark on the same product in remotely separate geographic areas. The key issue is that the junior user must not have had any knowledge of the senior use. Also, the two uses must not overlap geographically.[1]

So, when a large company (let's say they cover the whole nation) is planning on adopting a new identity, it must be very

cautious about the possibility of having a logo that is too much like that of a small local company somewhere out there. The small company (the senior user) would be able to prohibit the big firm (junior user) from using the new logo in the small company's market. From a practical point of view, the big firm would have to either: (1) change logos, or (2) more likely, pay the small firm a lot of money to acquire the logo rights. The best course of action is to avoid this altogether. (*See next page.*)

[1]Dorr and Munch, **Protecting Trade Secrets, Patents, Copyrights and Trademarks**, John Wiley & Sons, Inc., 1995, p. 124.

Names, Logos,
and secondary devices_____

Name used alone. The most likely way to avoid a legal problem with a logo is to simply use the name in type. For example, since the "Mythical Corporation" name has been around for many years, the use of the name alone is on sound legal ground. The design below may avoid legal problems, but it's bland and not memorable. As a marketing tool, it's very weak.

Mythical Corp.

Name with Logo. Many companies use the name along with a freestanding logo design. This is a much more creative way to show the company's identity, but there always lurks the possibility that your design is confusingly similar to that of another firm. The prospects of unintentionally choosing a "similar" logo are increased when the logo consists of a letter (such as the fanciful "M" shown below), or a common geometric shape (such as a diamond or circle, etc.) because there are a finite and limited number of letters and base geometric shapes from which to choose.

What happens when a company chooses a name/logo that conflicts with an existing company's name/logo? The senior user can be, and usually is, quite forceful requiring the junior user to change. For the small company, this might be as simple as changing stationery, a sign, and maybe a truck decal. For the huge company with thousands of items using the offending logo, the change may be quite costly—substantial costs of reprinting everything, OR having to buy out the rights to the trademark (in one case, this cost a large firm more than $500,000).

Name with Secondary Device. In recent years, the trend among global design firms has been to avoid the potential problems associated with the Name with Logo design. The common solution is to use a name which incorporates a secondary graphic device into the type (as opposed to a freestanding logo). In this style, type is the dominant element, and the "secondary device" is most often a modification of the type, or a graphic which has some interaction with the type. While there is no "100% safe" design from a legal standpoint, this option can present a strong corporate identity while having some degree of safety from the standpoint of trademark infringement problems.

Starting a Logo Project:
Important questions to ask _____

Enlightened by the attorney, the Mythical CEO called in a genuine corporate identity consulting firm, who was assigned the project. They began with these questions:

1. Does the current logo have any equity? (Equity may be defined as "residual value.") Some logos that are very outdated still have some qualities which should be retained in the new design. For example, an oval-shaped logo may be outdated, but the shape may be worth keeping.

In the Mythical logo, there is literally nothing that provides any equity.

2. What does the company see for its long-term future? With all its cash (from the sale of nonproductive fixed assets) Mythical intends to keep buying companies; there are no boundaries whatsoever in its plans. Mythical intends to become a "conglomerate"; this means that the logo cannot be product oriented.

3. Will the company be involved in multi-national communications? The global economy is here and now, even for many small firms. When a company markets across national (and cultural) borders, this must be considered, in company names as well as symbols.

A classic example of a good name that was destined for failure in another country is the Chevrolet Nova. That was a great name for the USA market, but in Spanish, Nova means "won't go."

4. Are there any legal implications to the name and/or the new logo? Just to be certain, the author had a trademark search done on the name "The Mythical Corporation." While there are several uses of the word "mythical" in corporate names in the USA, there was nothing found to be in conflict for using this name.

It is highly recommended that any firm that does business beyond state boundaries initiate a name search to prevent possible conflicts. Having a name that is too similar to that of another business can be expensive. A proper search can prevent these problems.

Also, if the logo is going to be used over a large part of the USA, there is also the potential for unknowingly coming up with a design that's already in use by someone else. See the two previous pages.

5. For major projects, the questions would be highly detailed, and might even involve several months of fact finding. Due to limited space, we'll keep it to one page.

Design parameters have two purposes: 1. make sure the design firm and the client agree on the project goals, and 2. keep the designers on track as they create.

A statement like this is highly useful in assuring that creativity is not wasted on concepts which are not valid.

ALSO: Before beginning any logo design project, it is good to review "What makes a good logo design" at right, and "Ten Mistakes to avoid" on pages xii & xiii.

Mythical
design parameters_____

Since the old Mythical logo is visually related to the firm's railroad days, there is absolutely no equity in the existing design.

The long-term plan of Mythical calls for acquiring existing companies and then changing the name of the firm to "Mythical", in order to build a strong brand equity across many industries.

In order to achieve this strong image for the Mythical name, it is mandatory that the Mythical name always be attached to a symbolic logo. (This assumes that there will be a logo that is not all type.)

Mythical's executives also want a logo that immediately stands out from the crowd. This may be done with design, color, or some combination thereof.

Since the Mythical name will appear in large size on buildings as well as in very small size on items such as watch dials, it is important that the new design work well when reproduced as small as 1/4-inch tall.

As this project is being done, Mythical has already acquired an airline, a car rental company, a hotel chain, and a golf resort, and wishes for the Mythical identity to appear on all appropriate items for these various new acquisitions. **Management is firm in its desire to change the name of each firm they acquire to "Mythical"; e.g. Mythical Car Rental, Mythical Bank, Mythical Airlines, etc.**

Mythical's corporate identity consulting firm has made a strong recommendation that the new identity be a design system, not just a logo design. That is, the new identity should be designed for effective use on items as diverse as:

- aircraft
- embossed into a bar of soap for the hotel group
- embroidered onto a uniform shirt.

The identity must work for the long term.
You can create a brochure that has a useful life of a few months, but corporate identity is too important (and expensive) to change with the seasons.

Corporate identity planning involves long-term thinking. The logo we are planning might be in use 20 years from now.

In summary, the new Mythical identity should be a distinctive, memorable design that projects a rapidly growing, world-class business.

What makes a good logo design

1. There is an identity **system**, not just a logo.

2. The logo must be original and distinctive.

3. The logo must be legible. (Many designs have a type face that is hard to read.)

4. The logo must be simple. (Too many designs are so complex that they defy explanation.)

5. The logo must be memorable. (Think of the Nike logo. Or IBM. Or McDonald's. Create something that sticks in the mind.)

6. The logo must be easily associated with the company.

7. The logo must work for all graphic media. (How will the design work on a business card?)

10 Mistakes

to avoid in logo design (mistakes on the left; effective solutions on the right) _____

1. **LINES ARE TOO THIN** _____
   Thin lines do not reproduce well. Avoid them.

2. **DEPENDS ON COLOR TO BE SUCCESSFUL** _____
   If the design **must** have color to be good—it isn't good.

3. **NEAR-ABSTRACT INITIAL FOR FIRST LETTER OF NAME** _____
   This tricky visual only confuses the reader.

4. **INAPPROPRIATE FOR THE TYPE OF BUSINESS** _____
   Don't try to be cute—be appropriate.

5. **WRONG PROPORTIONS FOR MOST USES** _____
   Marks which are extremely vertical or extremely horizontal will **not** work in most applications.

6. TOO BUSY _____
Remember that less is often more in terms of quality.

7. FAD TYPE FACE _____
A fad typeface will produce a design that is quickly out of date.

8. VISUAL CLICHES _____
Avoid the obvious solution.

9. COMPLETE LACK OF IMAGINATION (INCREDIBLY DULL) _____
Some "designs" show a lack of imagination.

10. GRADE-SCHOOL DESIGN (THE 6TH GRADE SOLUTION) _____
Professional designers always take the solution past Step 1.

Second
roughs _____

Using the design parameters which were established, the identity firm produced a number of
roughs which used the Mythical name in type, plus
a secondary device.

Some are shown below. (Many more were rejected
and not shown.)

Mythical
acquires Placebo_____

The morning after presenting the logos at left to Mythical management, the design team was having donuts and coffee as they read the financial news. They were shocked to see the article below.

Drunken Sailor?
Mythical Corporation Buys Drug Firm Placebo

———

Good for Mythical Finances, But What About Logo Project Now in Process?

———

By ROBERT DOLAN SMITH
Staff Reporter of THE MANTZ STREET JOURNAL

NEW YORK — The Mythical Corporation continued its spending spree by acquiring Placebo, Inc., the global drug manufacturer.

This is Mythical's fifth major acquisition this month, and some veteran financial analysts have compared the whirlwind gobbling up of top firms to a drunken sailor in port with six months worth of pay in his pocket.

Nonetheless, Mythical is quickly becoming a serious player in a variety of industries.

While Wall Street concentrates on the financial aspects of this newest acquisition, corporate identity experts are wondering what the Placebo acquisition will mean to the logo redesign project which is now in process.

According to insiders, Mythical was in the process of creating a single identity for all its units. The airline, car rental, hotel, and other divisions all would bear the name "Mythical." But since Placebo is one of the world's best known brand names, identity experts say it would be foolish to replace that name with Mythical.

Designers on the project were not available for comment.

This article caught the design team by surprise.

The concept of having every new acquisition adopt the Mythical name will probably be changed.

Before any more work is done on logos, we need to talk with the client.

Design Strategy
revision

The drug company, Placebo, never had a consistent logo. The firm simply used its name, set in some outline type, with a shadow background. Various styles of Bodoni or Cooper Bold were used, depending upon the whim of whoever was doing a particular project.

Placebo

Placebo

PLACEBO

Placebo

PLACEBO

Revised design strategy

The acquisition of one of the best-known brand names in the world has changed Mythical's plan of having a common name for all divisions.

The revised design strategy now includes these elements:

1. The Placebo name will be retained, but a new design is obviously needed.

2. The Placebo design must be something simple, as much of its potential market is in less developed nations, where literacy is low. (Research has shown that the name as shown is often pronounced improperly—often spoken as *place-bo*.)

3. While Placebo will retain its name, the Mythical management wants that name used in conjunction with Placebo—everywhere. "Why own a global brand if no one knows we own it?" they asked.

Presentation
of Placebo designs

Placebo

Pla ce bo

Placebo

Placebo

Placēbo

Pla•cē•bo

Final recommendation:
Mythical

Note that the logo is shown in both color and black and white. This should always be done before a final decision is made.

Since the logo will not always be printed in color (due to costs), the way it looks in black and white is very important to the overall identity.

This design was favored by the design firm for the following reasons:

1. It has an unusual secondary device, and the design aesthetics are very strong.

2. The "reverse italic" for the letter M is a characteristic that is rarely seen in identities. Another point for "unique."

3. The shape of the "y" is a pleasing transition between the reverse italic M and the italicized "thical."

4. The blue "underline" extends well beyond the end of the name—this may be used as a "balancing" effect for centering the logo.

5. Since the Mythical design is to be used as a "subordinate" mark to the Placebo design, it is strong enough to have good visibility even when shown in small sizes.

6. The red part of the secondary device, along with the M, is usable as a stand-alone graphic (in the future, when the design has become well established).

7. The blue "underline" can be extended upon occasion when the graphic would be enhanced by this effect.

Final recommendation:
Placebo

The Placebo mark will always be used with the Mythical identifier below it.

Note that the Mythical identifier is always equal in width to the width of the letters "ce·bo".

Pla·ce·bo
a **M**ythical company

This design was favored by the design firm for the following reasons:

1. The extended Placebo typeface creates a wide mark, allowing for the Mythical identifier below to be highly visible, without being dominant.

2. The secondary device visuals (pronunciation marks) are strong graphic identification, while being a guide on how to say the name correctly. The use of a secondary color makes these graphics strong symbols.

3. The design allows a maximum of two colors to be used in printing. Using two colors is very similar in cost to one-color printing. By comparison, process color can cost two or three times as much as black.

4. The design is easily adaptable to using different colors. The secondary color may be changed to indicate the different Placebo product lines.

Comments from the attorney

Both the Mythical and Placebo designs represent the "best of both worlds." That is, (1) the words and designs have been searched to be sure they do not conflict with any already-used mark; and (2) the logo and connecting secondary device are aesthetically pleasing to the consumer/viewer. The result is a proprietary mark that can be unique to the owner, such that when consumers see the mark in context, they think of only one company. Note that in the case of the tag line under Placebo, the goodwill associated with the parent Mythical is carried by the design and associated with Placebo, and vice versa.

Most corporate identity manuals are printed in limited quantities and appear in a 3-ring vinyl covered binder.

Following is the identity manual for the Mythical Corporation.

This is a very detailed, comprehensive manual. It includes materials typical of the best of the hundreds of manuals we studied for this book.

Mythical

Pla ce bo

a Mythical company

Introduction

Table of Contents

Note that there are "holes" shown at the inside edges on each page; this represents the look of holes punched into the pages that go into a typical 3-ring binder.

Also note that the pages in this "manual" are presented as both "left-hand" and "right-hand" pages. However, most manuals in binders are printed on one side only (resulting in "right-hand" pages), making changes and additions less costly.

Letter from the CEO

The typical manual has a set of tab dividers. To save space, we show only the one at right.

Most manuals have a letter from the CEO. This shows that top management is fully in support of the effort to assure a consistent identity.

To our employees and others who use our logo in the production of materials:

We take a great deal of pride in the corporate image which we have established. The new identity system for The Mythical Corporation and for Placebo was done in consultation with one of the world's premier corporate identity firms.

In order for us to get the maximum value from our new logos, we must have them used properly and consistently.

This manual is to be used as the single source to answer the question "how should our logo be used" on a large variety of items.

In order to make this process easier, we have enclosed a Macintosh® disk which includes the information from each page in this manual. All you need to do in order to get letterheads printed, for example, is take the disk to a qualified printer. For personalized items such as business cards, the specifications are in place; all you have to do is insert the name and title to be printed.

Much of our future growth is dependent upon having the corporate image which we desire. By adhering to the standards in this manual, you will have us move in the right direction.

When you have questions about any application of our corporate identity, call the graphics coordinator at extension 545 for clarification.

Sincerely,

David E. Carter
Chief Executive Officer

Yes, it's the same guy who wrote this book. If I can make up a mythical firm, I get to be CEO.

Using the Templates on the CD-ROM

Most of the pages in this manual include a template showing some object or item on which the Mythical or Placebo logo will appear. The truck below is an example of such a template.

EVERY template in this book is on the accompanying CD-ROM.

The CD that comes with this book contains approximately 350 templates, such as the truck above. These templates are in EPS form for both Macintosh and PC applications.

On each page, type at the bottom left shows the name of the template.

The back of the book shows additional templates on the CD which do not appear in the Mythical manual.

These templates are all blank (with no logo).

If this had been an actual manual, the CD would include all the logo applications shown in this book, and would be ready for use by printers, sign producers, etc.

This "identity manual on a disk" is a relatively new concept, but is very efficient, as it virtually eliminates the potential for having a supplier produce the logo in an improper way.

V-02 truck

The Mythical Logo—Corporate

The Mythical logo is shown here in its standard form for corporate use. The logo may be used only in these two forms:

black and white, and as a 3-color design.

Position guidelines: The Mythical logo features an "underline" which extends to the right beyond the type. When this logo is placed for use, this must be "balanced" with an equal amount of "white space" at the left of the logo.

The box at right shows the amount of horizontal space taken up by the "underline."

The logo must be placed so that there is equal "white space" at the left of the logo (represented by the left box).

The alignment for visual center is indicated by the dotted line.

The Mythical Logo—Alternates

In order to identify the various Mythical divisions, it is sometimes necessary to attach a word (such as "Airlines" or "Bank") to the Mythical logo. This is especially true for signage and some forms.

The Mythical logo may have several forms:

Various applications of these various logos are shown in this manual.

This system will allow for expansion into new areas; the words may change, but the system is to be followed for future acquisitions.

1. Mythical standard logo.

2. Mythical logo with extended underline.

3. Mythical logo with division descriptor below.

4. Mythical logo with division descriptor at right.

5. Mythical logo with division descriptor at right and details at bottom.

The Placebo Logo

The Placebo logo is normally used in conjunction with the Mythical identity line ("A Mythical company") underneath. The standard format for this is shown directly below. Note that the identity line fits within the space used by the letters "ce•bo" as noted in the example at the bottom of the page. No other space and size relationship between these two elements is permitted. The type elements are always in black. The •-• graphic within the logo is always in color. (See colors on pages 7 & 11.)

Pla•ce•bo
a **Mythical** company

Pla•ce•bo
a **Mythical** company

The Placebo logo has many possible color variations. One use of various colors is to indicate different products. Since much of the market for Placebo products is in developing countries where it is difficult to get consistent results in color printing, there is no specific color that is required for use on the • - • graphic.

Type Standards

Versions of New Baskerville are used to create Mythical logos, while versions of Sans Extended make up the Placebo logo. These two font families may be used with its originating logo, but judgment should be exercised so printed materials with much text do not look boring.

On page 5, Mythical logos style #3 and #4 with division descriptors below and beside, respectively, utilize New Baskerville, all caps, at 90% width for the descriptors. Black is preferred for descriptors at bottom, corporate blue for descriptors to the right of the standard Mythical logo.

The Mythical logo style #5 with descriptor at right and details at bottom use New Baskerville. The descriptor to the right is all lowercase with only regular kerning between the standard Mythical logo and descriptor—not word spacing—and in corporate blue. On the bottom, "and" is New Baskerville, lowercase, and black. Details are New Baskerville bold, all caps set at 85% width in corporate red.

Palatino should be used for body copy when materials have more than five lines of text—such as this Graphic Standards Manual.

The following font families are permissible to use in association with the Mythical and Placebo logos: Aquitaine Initials ICG, Balmoral ICG, GimletSSi, New Baskerville, and Palatino. In addition, the Sans Extended DTC family may be utilized with Placebo materials.

New Baskerville Roman
ABCDEFGHIJKLMNOPQRSTUVWXYZ abcdefghijklmnopqrstuvwxyz
0123456789

New Baskerville Roman italic
ABCDEFGHIJKLMNOPQRSTUVWXYZ abcdefghijklmnopqrstuvwxyz
0123456789

New Baskerville Bold
ABCDEFGHIJKLMNOPQRSTUVWXYZ abcdefghijklmnopqrstuvwxyz
0123456789

New Baskerville Bold italic
ABCDEFGHIJKLMNOPQRSTUVWXYZ abcdefghijklmnopqrstuvwxyz
0123456789

Aquitaine Initials ICG
ABCDEFGHIJKLMNOPQRSTUVWXYZ
ABCDEFGHIJKLMNOPQRSTUVWXYZ 0123456789

Aquitaine Initials ICG alternate
ABCDEFGHIJKLMNOPQRSTUVWXYZ
ABCDEFGHIJKLMNOPQRSTUVWXYZ 0123456789

Balmoral ICG
ABCDEFGHIJKLMNOPQRSTUVWXYZ
abcdefghijklmnopqrstuvwxyz 0123456789

GimletSSi
ABCDEFGHIJKLMNOPQRSTUVWXYZ
abcdefghijklmnopqrstuvwxyz 0123456789

Gimlet Light SSi
ABCDEFGHIJKLMNOPQRSTUVWXYZ
abcdefghijklmnopqrstuvwxyz 0123456789

Palatino
ABCDEFGHIJKLMNOPQRSTUVWXYZ
abcdefghijklmnopqrstuvwxyz 0123456789

Sans Extended Regular DTC
ABCDEFGHIJKLMNOPQRSTUVWXYZ
abcdefghijklmnopqrstuvwxyz 0123456789

Sans Light Extended Regular DTC
ABCDEFGHIJKLMNOPQRSTUVWXYZ
abcdefghijklmnopqrstuvwxyz 0123456789

Color Standards—Mythical

The Mythical logo is in red, blue, and black. It is important that the exact colors of red and blue are used to reproduce the logo. While there are many color systems available for printing, we have found that it is best to use a basic mixture of standard 4-color inks. The Mythical colors are shown below, along with their formulae.

Mythical Red

100% magenta
100% yellow

Mythical Blue

100% cyan
100% magenta

Note about colors: The Mythical colors are shown here printed on "coated" paper. When the same exact ink is printed on a paper that is not coated, it will have a slightly different color. It is important that you are aware that paper texture and quality have an effect upon the final outcome of color inks.

Many designers show logos along with a "color chip" from a color spec book.

Most often, they use a chip that has a "C" after the color number, as the color is brighter and prettier than the "U" chips. This "C" means that the paper is coated; "U" stands for uncoated. Showing a "C" chip when the job will be printed on a letterhead, for example, is going to produce a result that is somewhat different than was expected.

The Placebo logo is in black and a secondary color for the • - • graphic. Since there is no rigid system for the second color, no specifications are presented here.

However, the one basic rule for choosing a secondary color is: the color mix should include no more than 35% black on a standard 4-color process ink (CMYK) system.

Pla•cē•bo
a M̲ythical company

This block has:

100% magenta
35% black

Acceptable

This block has:

12% cyan
100 % magenta
100% yellow
40% black

NOT Acceptable — too dark

Mythical

Corporate Headquarters
3561 My Way
Lanier, Illinois 57250
Phone 555-555-4678 • Fax 555-555-4680

The letterhead, card, and envelope are shown here on a single page.

If this were a real manual, the Macintosh disk would include a document for each item, probably in both Macromedia FreeHand and Quark XPress.

Mythical

BUSTER D. MATIAN
Art Director

Corporate Headquarters
3561 My Way
Lanier, Illinois 57250
Phone 555-555-4678 • Fax 555-555-4680

Mythical

Corporate Headquarters
3561 My Way
Lanier, Illinois 57250

Executives at the level of vice president and above may use stationery which is embossed as well as engraved. These examples show the correct configuration: blind embossed Mythical logo, with the address information engraved in black ink. Note that the executive stationery is in ivory, while standard stationery is white.

Mythical

Corporate Headquarters
3561 My Way
Lanier, Illinois 57250
Phone 555-555-4678 • Fax 555-555-4680

Mythical

LAUREN L. CARTER
Executive Vice President

Corporate Headquarters
3561 My Way
Lanier, Illinois 57250
Phone 555-555-4678 • Fax 555-555-4680

Mythical

Corporate Headquarters
3561 My Way
Lanier, Illinois 57250

Stationery—Mythical

Personal handwritten notes from executives should be on Mythical monarch size stationery. This ivory stock matches the executive stationery color. The monarch size letter includes only the

Mythical logo blind embossed into the paper. The envelope includes the Mythical logo embossed into the flap on the back of the envelope; while the address is engraved in black.

Corporate Headquarters
3561 My Way
Lanier, Illinois 57250

The Placebo corporate stationery includes the logo
in black and violet on a gray stock.

Pla•cē•bo
a **M**ythical company
44 Beauchamp Place • London, WI V9DC
171- 900-9000
Fax:171-900-9009

Not long ago, the statio-
nery pages in manuals had
precise details on size
of logo (in mm), size of
type, and how far down
and how far in (also in
mm) each type block was
to be positioned.

Now, this is not needed.
Manuals which include
stationery templates on
disk or CD-ROM take away
the element of chance
when producing statio-
nery.

Pla•cē•bo
a **M**ythical company

44 Beauchamp Place
London, WI V9DC
171- 900-9000   **CHRISTA A. CARTER**
Fax:171-900-9009   Managing Director

Pla•cē•bo
a **M**ythical company
44 Beauchamp Place • London, WI V9DC

Stationery—Placebo

Placebo Executives at the level of vice president and above may use stationery which is embossed as well as engraved. These examples show the correct configuration: blind embossed Placebo logo, with the address information engraved in black ink.

NOTE: the tag line " a Mythical company" should be engraved in black ink, as it is too small to be embossed and show up properly.

Placcebo
a **M**ythical company
44 Beauchamp Place • London, WIV9DC
171- 900-9000
Fax: 171-900-9009

Placcebo
a **M**ythical company

44 Beauchamp Place
London, WIV9DC
171- 900-9000
Fax: 171-900-9009

Linda G. Carter
Vice President

Placcebo
a **M**ythical company
44 Beauchamp Place • London, WI V9DC

Personal handwritten notes from executives should be on Placebo monarch size stationery. The monarch size letter includes only the Placebo logo blind embossed into the paper. The envelope includes the Placebo logo embossed into the flap on the back of the envelope while the address is engraved in black. (Note: this is one of the few examples where the Placebo logo does not include the line "a Mythical company."

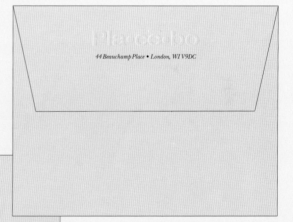

44 Beauchamp Place • London, WI V9DC

Mythical Forms

The preferred configuration for all Mythical forms is for the standard Mythical logo to be used. Whenever possible, the Mythical logo is to be as far left as possible, and near the top of the form. (However, the logo is not to be nearer than 1/4 inch to the edge of a form.)

Mythical

INVOICE

Corporate Headquarters
3561 My Way
Lanier, Illinois 57250-6167
Phone 555-555-4678 • Fax 555-555-4680

no. _____

date _____

Sold to:

Qty.	Description	Unit

Ship

Balan

Terms: all invoices are due Net 10 days from r

Mythical

PURCHASE ORDER

Corporate Headquarters
3561 My Way
Lanier, Illinois 57250-6167
Phone 555-555-4678 • Fax 555-555-4680

PO no. _____

vendor no. _____

date _____

Vendor:

Qty.	Description	Unit Price	Net Price

Shipping & Handling

Balance Due

Terms _____

All Mythical checks include the 3-color corporate logo, even when payment is for items purchased by operating divisions. All Mythical checks are to have a background that includes the Mythical logo in a 10% grey, and repeated to form a background shown in the example below. This design is for both identity and security purposes.

Mythical

Corporate Headquarters
3561 My Way • Lanier, Illinois 57250
(555) 555-4678

1,111,111

date _____

pay to the
order of _____ $ _____

_____ dollars

memo _____   _____

Placebo Forms

The preferred configuration for all Placebo forms is for the Placebo logo with the line "a Mythical company" to be placed as far to the left as possible on the form, and near the top of the form. (However, the logo is not to be nearer than 1/4 inch to the edge of a form.)

Pla•cē•bo
a **M**ythical company

44 Beauchamp Place • London, WI 00100
Phone 171- 900-9000 • Fax: 171-900-9009

INVOICE

no. _____

date _____

Sold to:

Qty.   Description   Unit

Shipp

Balan

Terms: all invoices are due Net 10 days from r

Pla•cē•bo
a **M**ythical company

44 Beauchamp Place • London, WI 00100
Phone 171- 900-9000 • Fax: 171-900-9009

PURCHASE ORDER

PO no. _____

vendor no. _____

date _____

Vendor:

Qty.	Description	Unit Price	Net Price

Shipping & Handling

Balance Due

Terms _____

All Placebo checks include the 2-color corporate logo. All Placebo checks are to have a background that includes the Placebo logo (including the line, "a Mythical company") in a 10% grey, and re- peated to form a background shown in the ex- ample below. This design is for both identity and security purposes.

Trucks

When used on vehicles, the preferred configuration of the Mythical logo is for the end of the underline to extend to the farthest possible point to the right.

Note that the "white space" to the left of the logo is equal in width to the underline past the Mythical name.

For the backs of tractor trailers, the preferred configuration of the Mythical logo is like the side view: the end of the underline extends to the farthest possible point to the right.

Again, note that the "white space" to the left of the logo is equal in width to the underline past the Mythical name.

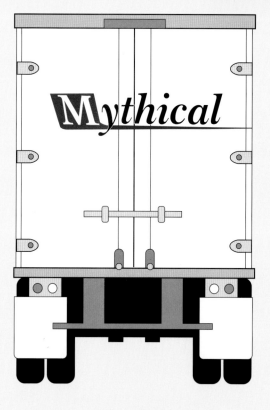

Note the template names at lower left.

You can create your own manuals by using the templates on the CD-ROM that comes with this book.

V-02 truck
V-04a truck back

For the tandem trailer, the Mythical logo is used in a modified form—the underline extends from the front trailer to the back.

For tractor trailers with a roll-up back, make sure that the logo is placed within one division and not across a separating hinge.

Again, note that the "white space" to the left of the logo is equal in width to the underline past the Mythical name.

V-06 truck
V-04b truckback

Trucks

Normally, the end of the Mythical underline would extend to the farthest possible point to the right. However, this tanker has a ladder which changes the visual perception of the unit as a whole. In addition, there is no "line" where the side ends—rather the vessel is rounded at the back. In cases like this, the underline is to be placed at an aesthetically pleasing point near the back of the tanker.

For the backs of tanker trucks, the preferred configuration of the Mythical logo is like the side view: the end of the underline extends to the farthest possible point to the right.

Again, note that the "white space" to the left of the logo is equal in width to the underline past the Mythical name.

V-08 tanker
V-05 tankback

When used on vehicles, the preferred configuration of the Mythical logo is for the end of the underline to extend to the farthest possible point to the right.

Note that the "white space" to the left of the logo is equal in width to the underline past the Mythical name.

For proper use of the Mythical logo on the back of delivery trucks, see page 22.

V-10 truck

Trucks

When used on vehicles, the preferred configuration of the Mythical logo is for the end of the underline to extend to the farthest possible point to the right.

Note that the "white space" to the left of the logo is equal in width to the underline past the Mythical name.

For proper use of the Mythical logo on the back of delivery trucks, see page 22.

V-09 truck

When used on vehicles, the preferred configuration of the Mythical logo is for the end of the underline to extend to the farthest possible point to the right.

Note that the "white space" to the left of the logo is equal in width to the underline past the Mythical name.

For proper use of the Mythical logo on the back of delivery trucks, see page 22.

V-14 truck

Trucks

The door panels, handles, etc., of this vehicle
prevent getting a smooth application of the logo.
In cases like this, it is permissible to use the
Mythical logo variation where the logo underline
is extremely elongated.

For proper use of the Mythical logo on the back of
delivery trucks, see page 22.

V-15 truck

When used on vehicles, the preferred configuration of the Mythical logo is for the end of the underline to extend to the farthest possible point to the right.

Note that the "white space" to the left of the logo is equal in width to the underline past the Mythical name.

For proper use of the Mythical logo on the back of delivery trucks, see page 22.

V-12 truck

Trucks

When used on vehicles, the preferred configuration of the Mythical logo is for the end of the underline to extend to the farthest possible point to the right.

Note that the "white space" to the left of the logo is equal in width to the underline past the Mythical name.

For proper use of the Mythical logo on the back of trucks, see page 22.

V-22 dump truck

Some vehicles have extended panels which make it difficult to get a painted or decal image to appear properly. In these cases, the truck door is the preferred location for the logo.

When the truck door is used for the logo, the underline is to extend to the edge of the cab. The left side of the logo will have a large area of white space, so it is not necessary to center the design on the door.

For dump truck backs, the Mythical logo is to have the underline extend to the extreme right edge of the back panel.

V-21 dump truck
V-23a dumpback

Trucks

Since pickup trucks do not have a large display area at the back the way larger trucks do, the Mythical logo is to be placed on the door panel.

The Mythical underline is to extend to the right edge of the cab. The left side of the logo may end near the door crease, since there is a large amount of white space at left.

For pickup truck backs, the Mythical logo is to be placed so that the underline extends to the right edge of the panel.

V-25 pickup
V-23b pickup back

When used on vehicles, the preferred configuration of the Mythical logo is for the end of the underline to extend to the farthest possible point to the right.

Note that the "white space" to the left of the logo is equal in width to the underline past the Mythical name.

For proper use of the Mythical logo on the back of delivery trucks, see page 22.

V-20 step van

Trucks

When used on panel van vehicles, the preferred configuration of the Mythical logo is for the end of the underline to extend to the farthest possible point to the right.

Note that the "white space" to the left of the logo is equal in width to the underline past the Mythical name.

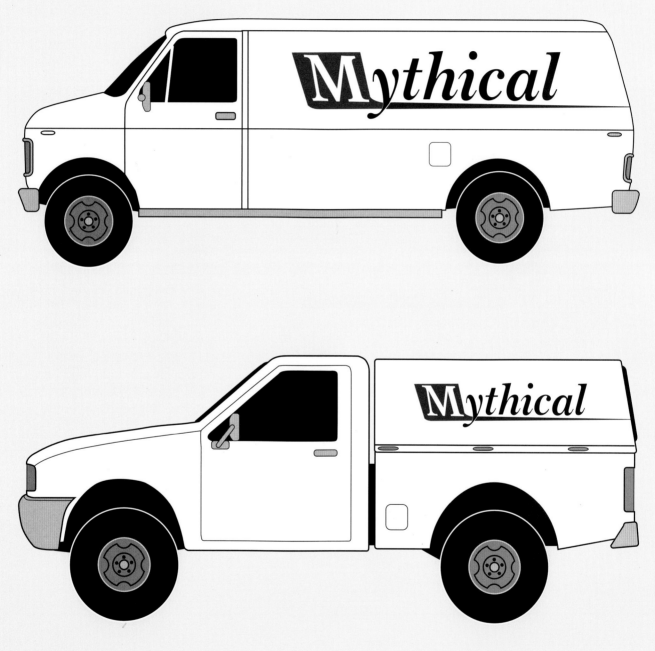

V-32 van
V-29 pickup

On automobiles, the Mythical logo is always to be placed on the door panel. Since the normal "truck" size logo would be gaudy, the automobile standard is to have the logo centered, and covering approximately half of the width of the door.

V-36 car

Busses

On busses, the Mythical logo should be as large as it can be, within the bounds of good taste. Two different configurations are shown here. Obviously, it is not always feasible to have the underline extend to the edge of a vehicle, especially with busses.

V-41 bus
V-40 bus

Forklifts have a limited amount of space for logos.
Since various brands of these vehicles have
different styles, the logo should go in the largest
space available, and the underline should extend
to a right edge whenever possible.

V-24 forklift

Golf Carts

Golf carts have a limited amount of space for logos. Since various brands of these vehicles have different styles, the logo should go in the largest space available, and the underline should extend to a right edge whenever possible.

V-43 golfcart

It is difficult to formulate a set of logo application rules for railcars and watercraft due to their great diversity.

For the diesel engine shown below, the Mythical logo is to be placed in the largest available area, and with the standard rules applying: the underline goes to the right edge (the visual edge, in this case) with an equal amount of white space to the left of the logo.

RW-05 engine

Railcars

Although there is a large open space on this engine, the Mythical logo does not fill the entire area since it would be too overpowering. For the diesel engine shown below, the Mythical logo is to be placed in the largest area, but it takes up only about 1/3 of the space.

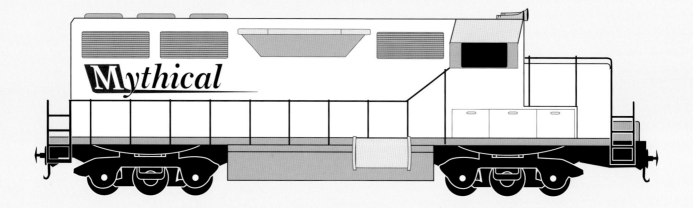

RW-06 engine

Although there is a large open space on this engine, the Mythical logo does not fill the entire area since it would be too overpowering. For the diesel engine shown below, the Mythical logo is to be placed in the largest area, but it takes up only about 1/3 of the space.

Rail cars of various types have many possible logo positions. However, to establish a rule — such as "all logos on the right side" is not possible.

So — there is some lee-way on where to place logos on the Mythical rail cars. Here, the logo could be centered, at left, or at right. The important thing is that all similar cars have the logo in a consistent location.

RW-01 passenger

Railcars

Although there is a large open space on this passenger car, the Mythical logo does not fill the entire area. In this case, the size of the logo is limited by the height available under the windows.

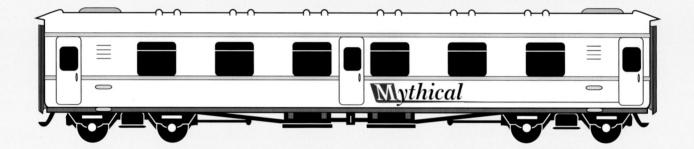

RW-02 passenger

Although there is a large open space on this tanker car, the Mythical logo does not fill the entire area. In this case, the size of the logo is limited by the ladder at left. The Mythical logo is centered on the tanker, with the left side limitation imposed by the ladder.

RW-03 tank

Railcars

Although there is a large open space on this boxcar, the Mythical logo does not fill the entire area. In this case, the size of the logo is limited by the doors at right. Note that the underline ends at the edge of the doors, while there is compensating white space at the left of the logo.

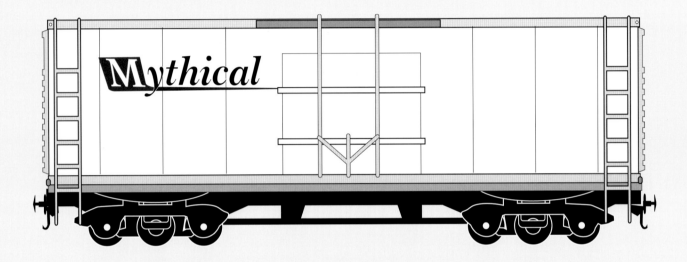

RW-07 boxcar

Although there is a very large open space on this boxcar, the Mythical logo does not fill the entire area. The logo covers no more than 1/3 of the total horizontal space available.

RW-08 boxcar

Railcars

Although there is a large open space on this coal
car, the Mythical logo does not fill the entire area.
Note that the underline ends at the edge of the car,
while there is compensating white space at the left
of the logo.

RW-09 bucketcar

There is minimal logo space on this tug. The most obvious place for a logo is the smokestack, with another logo on the side of the bow. Note that the underline goes all the way to the right of the smokestack. The logo on the bow is aligned with the curvature of the vessel.

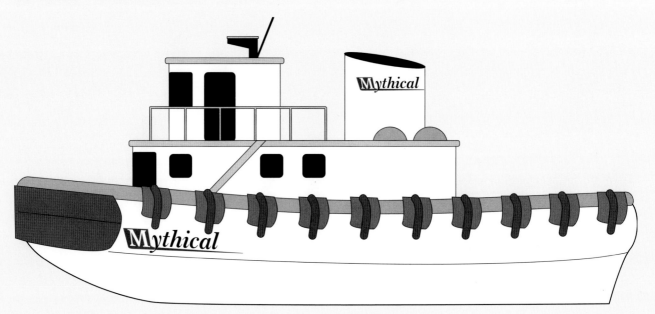

RW-16 tug

Watercraft

This barge has as much display space as several billboards—but much of the time, it is underwater like an iceberg.

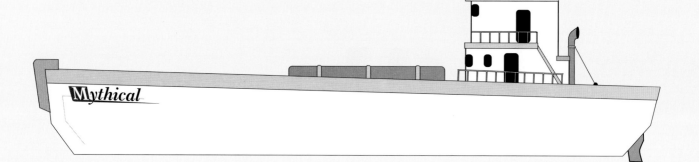

RW-15 barge

This cargo ship has a lot of visual space, but it is so elongated that the Mythical logo can take up only a small part of the huge wall. Note that the angle of the logo has been changed to match the shape of the vessel.

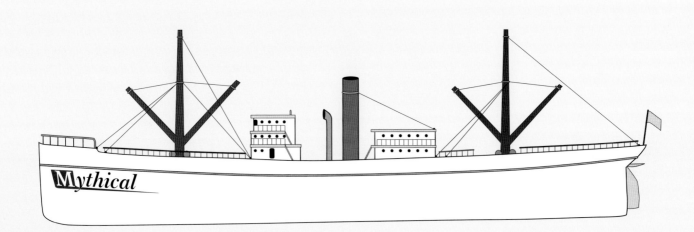

RW-13 lg cargo

Watercraft

This tanker has a huge space available, but it is highly horizontal so the Mythical logo will fit on only a small part of the front section. Note that the logo has been aligned with the angle of the profile of the ship.

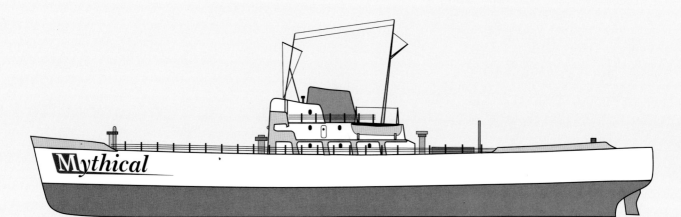

RW-12 freight

This freighter has a huge space available, but it is totally underwater when filled to capacity. So, the Mythical logo is positioned at the bow to be well above the high water mark. Note that the logo is aligned with the profile of the vessel.

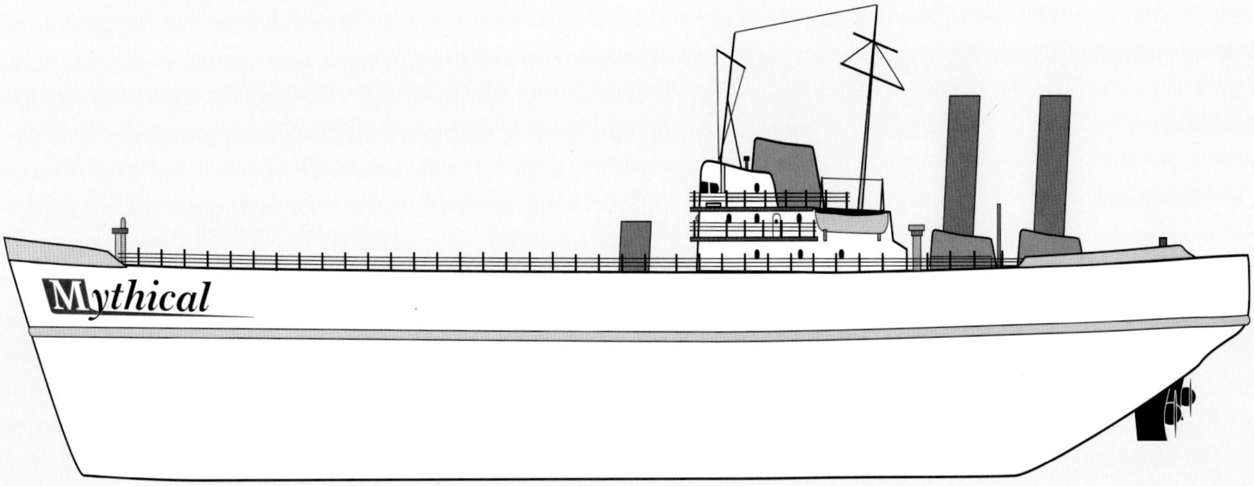

Mythical

RW-11 tanker

Watercraft

This cruise ship is a great opportunity to have the Mythical logo displayed to thousands of people daily. The design is placed at the bow, as large as possible, and angled to match the shape of the ship.

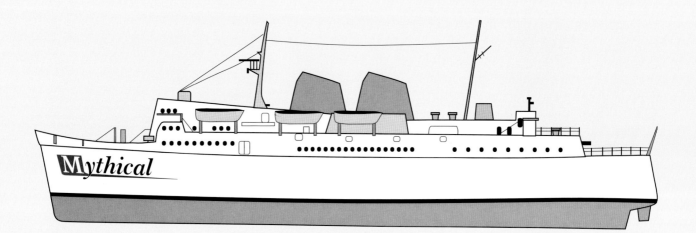

RW-10 cruise

This yacht has the Mythical logo in a vertical position on its largest sail. Note that the underline goes off the edge of the sail while there is compensating white space at the other end.

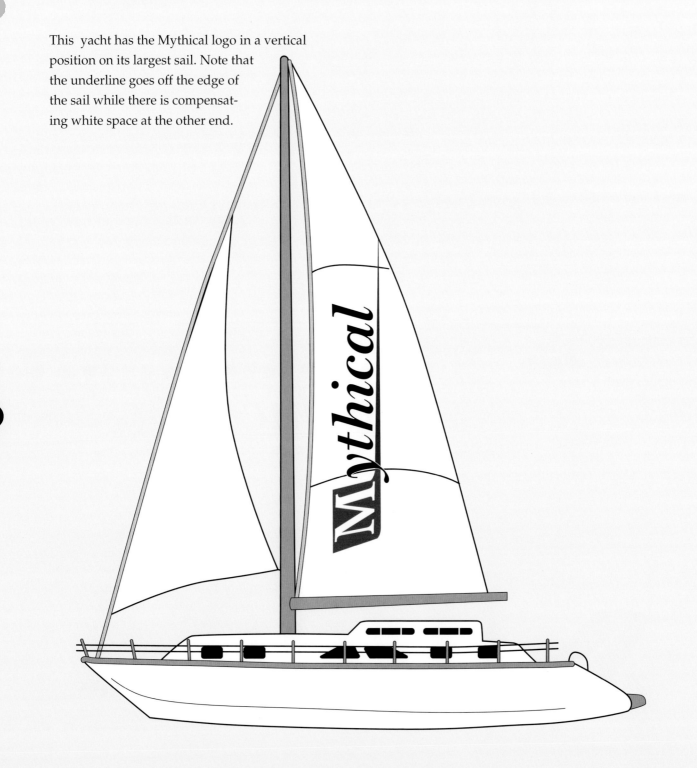

RW-17 yacht

General rules for aircraft: The Mythical logo is to appear near the front of the aircraft. On the left side, it should begin below, but in alignment with, the first passenger window and extend as far as possible toward the wing. (This is comparable to the logo extending to the edge of trucks.) The left edge of the logo begins very near the edge of the main door. (There is plenty of white space at the left.)

Since there is a wide variety of aircraft configurations, there cannot be total consistency in use of the Mythical logo. This section covers most of the logo applications for aircraft currently in use by the company.

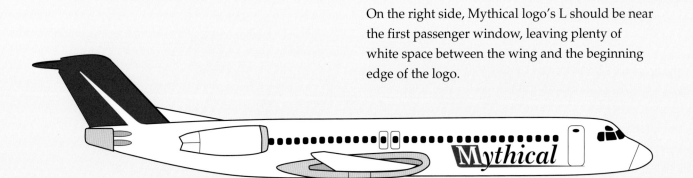

On the right side, Mythical logo's L should be near the first passenger window, leaving plenty of white space between the wing and the beginning edge of the logo.

A-26 FokkerF28

In many manuals, double-sized, fold-out pages are used to show especially large items, such as aircraft, rail cars, etc. The airliners in this section are presented in that format.

Rules for Mythical Airlines Tail Graphic

All Mythical Airlines planes have a standard tail graphic—a corporate blue background with a white element flowing upward. The angle of the back portion of the white element is to be in alignment with the leading edge of the tail.

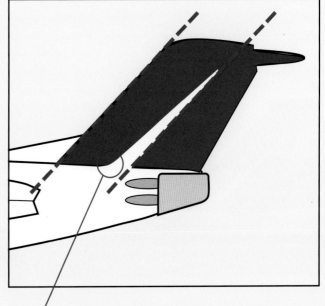

The base of the front of the white element is to be slightly rounded.

Mythical's logo in this case follows the general rule of beginning below, but in alignment with, the first passenger window and extending as far as possible toward the wing. Special allowance has been made, however, with the angling of the logo so it's almost parallel with the aircraft's belly.

On the right side, the Mythical logo is visually centered between the wing and front edge of the plane.

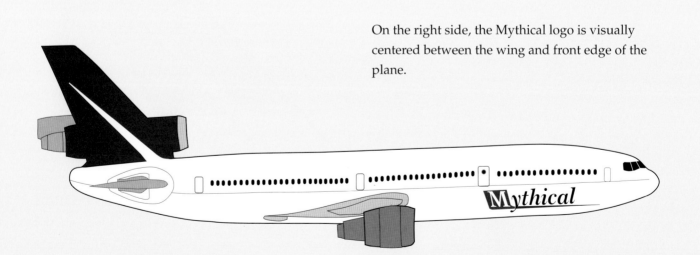

A-08 DC10

The tail of the plane can make a large display area for the logo, and many airlines use this highly effectively.

However, tread carefully. The angle of this area is different on most aircraft. For example, a logo design that was very appropriate for the top aircraft, would not work on a different tail design.

Notice how the two aircraft tails below have greatly different angles. The bottom design is angled so much that it bears little similarity to the one on top.

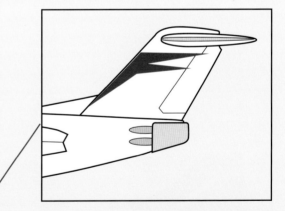

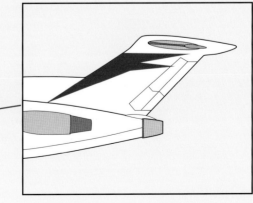

The Concorde aircraft is the world's fastest passenger plane. Its sleek profile presents a problem for logo placement. For the Concorde, the logo begins with front door's edge and the underline extends to the wing.

For the Concorde, the logo begins just under the front windows and the underline extends to just under the front door.

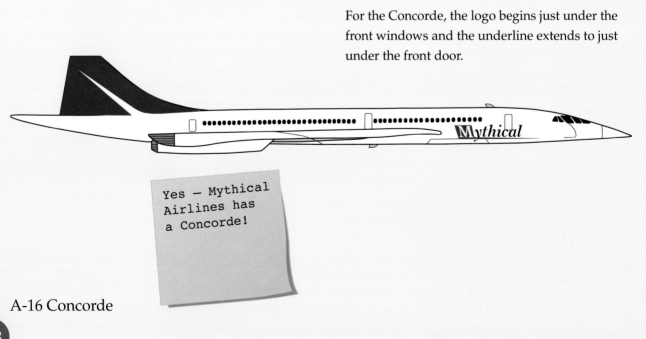

Yes — Mythical Airlines has a Concorde!

A-16 Concorde

Most designers will never get a chance to design an identity system for an airline. However, this is a great student project to force the design of a system -- not a logo.

There are so many different aircraft configurations that a lot of thought must go into the planning of how the logo will be used. . .before the final design is created.

You can learn a lot from this section, no matter what type project you do.

OK, so you'll never get a chance to design an identity system for an airline, but there are a lot of companies with corporate aircraft, and here's where a lot of designers will get to use some of what this chapter teaches.

The corporate aircraft begin on manual page 79.

Don't forget that aircraft have two sides.

The great logo here for "Flaming Airways" is a nice image on the plane's left side. . .

. . .but when it's on the right, the "flipped" design doesn't communicate the letter "F".

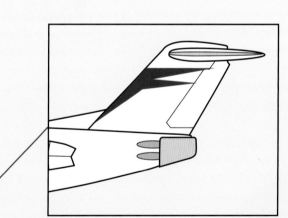

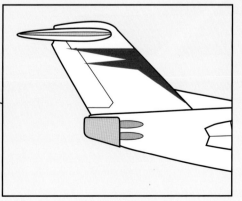

The Lockheed 1011 is a widebody aircraft that is used on intercontinental flights. The Mythical logo is to begin under and in alignment with the front window's edge, and extend the underline to the wing position.

On the right side, the Mythical logo is centered between the front two doors.

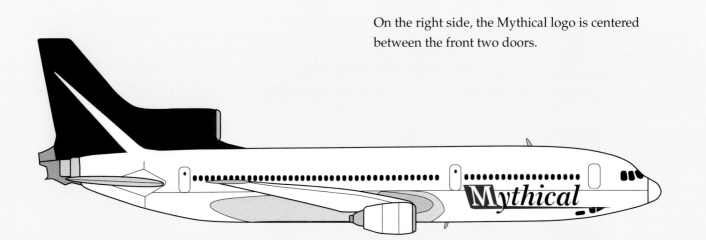

A-29 L1011

Note how well the Mythical tail graphic works on a wide range of aircraft configurations.

The MD90 aircraft is so elongated in its profile that the standard corporate logo cannot extend from the front door to the wing position. In this case, the logo is to begin at the front window's edge, and simply extend to its normal size with no effort made to have the underline meet the wing.

On the right side, the logo's L should be near the first passenger window.

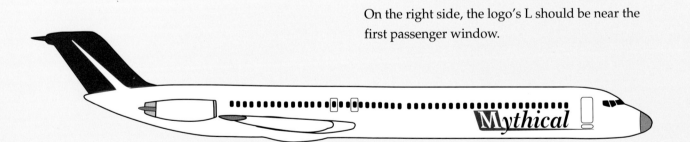

A-15 MD90

Aircraft

The Boeing 737 has a shorter, stockier profile than many planes. In addition, the presence of an engine on the wing blocks part of the standard logo position from view. The logo is to be near the front window edge, and the underline extends to the wing (even though it is not visible due to the engine.)

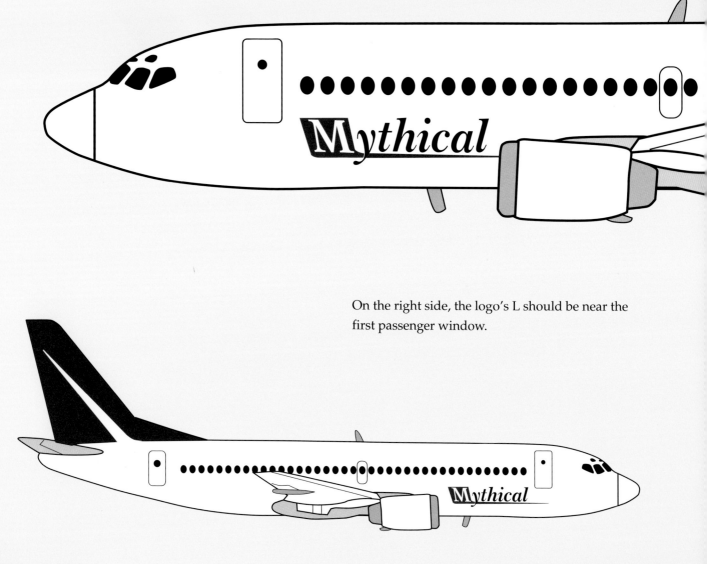

On the right side, the logo's L should be near the first passenger window.

A-33 B737

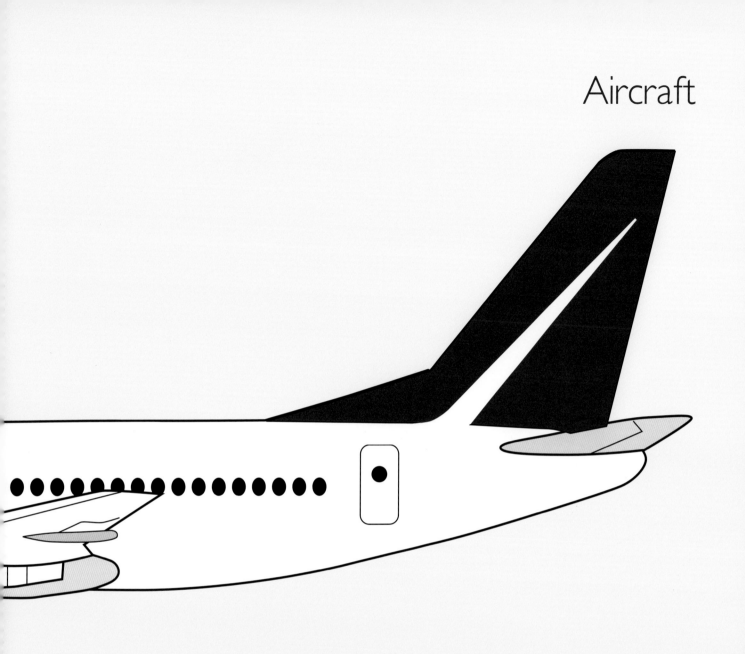

The Boeing 727 uses the Mythical logo in its
standard position beginning at the window, and
extending to the wing position.

The Mythical logo's L is near the first passenger
window on the right side.

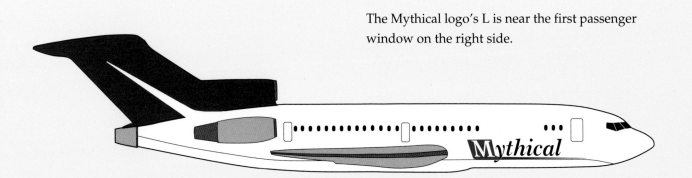

A-09 B727

The third engine on the 727 makes the background color even stronger.

This is an example of: designing a system, not just a logo."

The Boeing 767 aircraft is to use the standard Mythical logo in its front position, beginning at the front window and extending to the wing position.

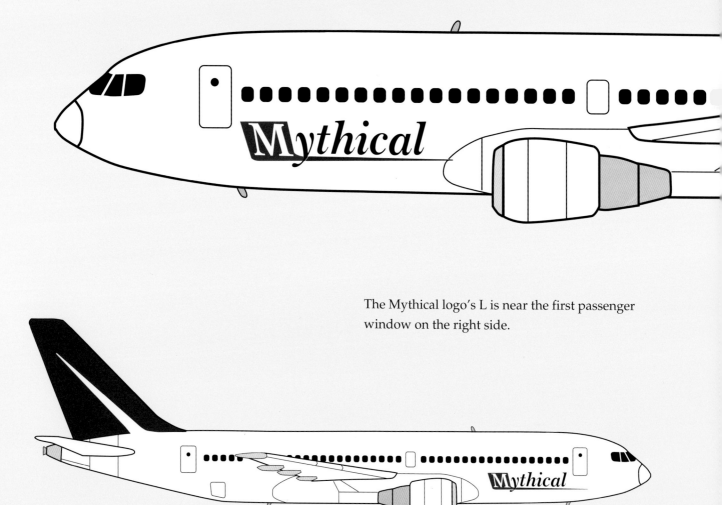

The Mythical logo's L is near the first passenger window on the right side.

A-31 B767

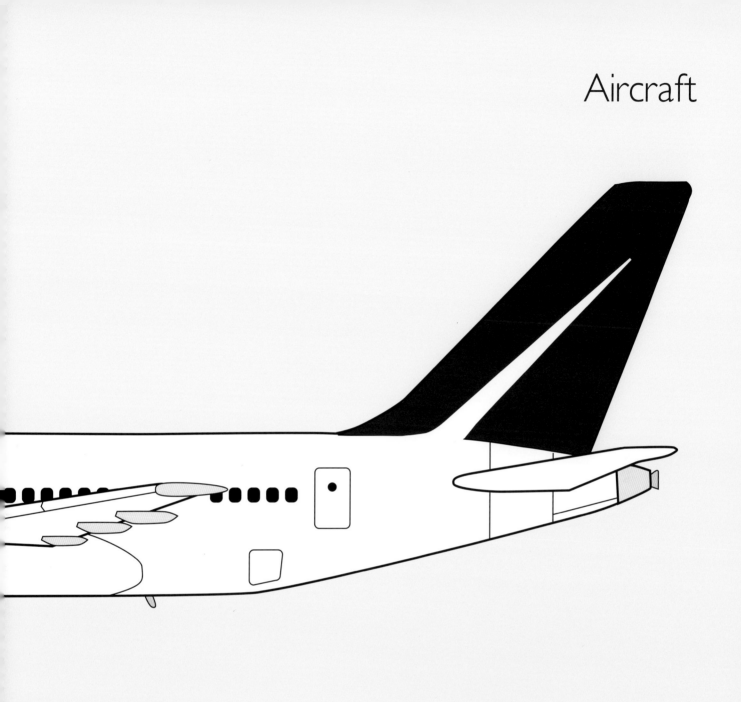

Aircraft

The Boeing 777 aircraft is to use the standard Mythical logo in its front position, beginning at the front window.

The Mythical logo's L is near the first passenger window on the right side.

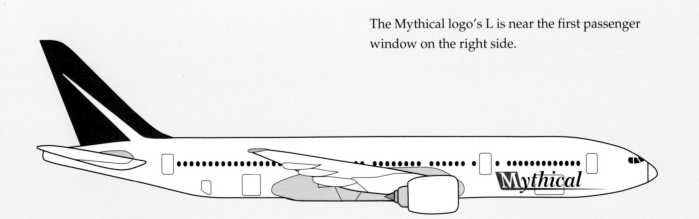

A-30 B777

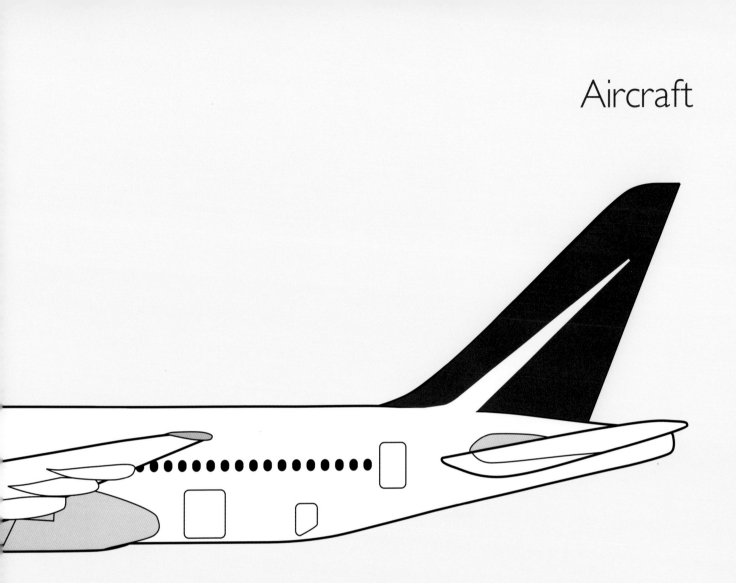

The Boeing 757 aircraft is to use the standard Mythical logo in its front position, beginning at the front window.

The Mythical logo's L is near the first passenger window on the right side.

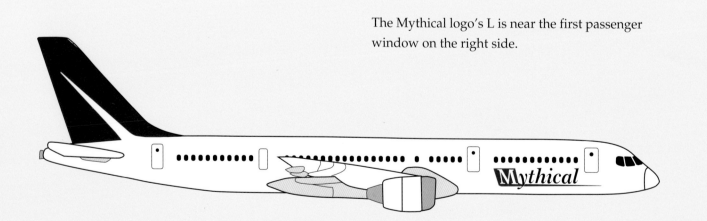

A-32 B757

Aircraft

The Boeing 747 aircraft has a profile unlike any other aircraft. The "hump" near the front actually includes a "second story" to the passenger section. This configuration makes it necessary to change the logo position to a location over the standard windows, and behind the hump.

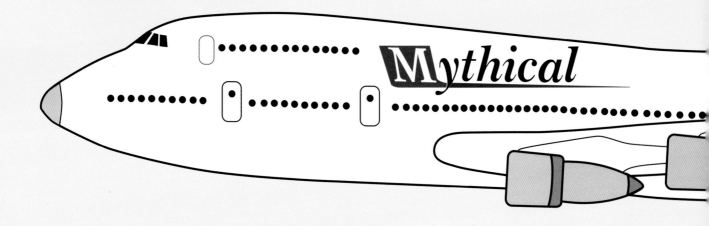

The logo position in this case is similar to that on the left side of the aircraft— over the standard windows, and behind the hump.

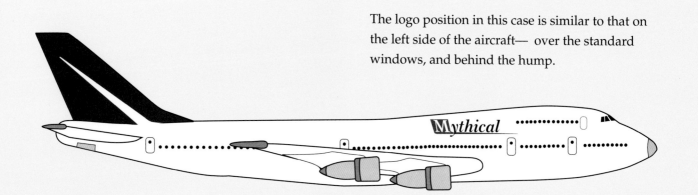

A-05 B747-400

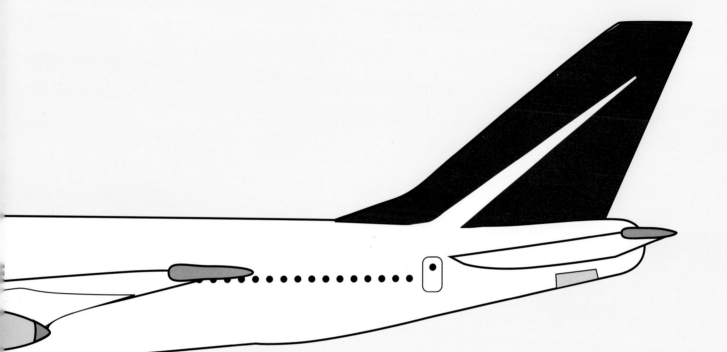

Aircraft

The BA111 uses the Mythical logo that begins near the front window and extends the underline to the wing position.

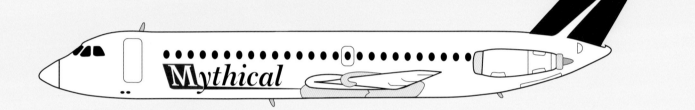

On the right side, again the logo's L should be near the front window.

A-28 BA111

This DC-3 is virtually an "antique" aircraft, but it is still flown by small airlines in countries around the world.

Due to its unusual configuration (it has a tail wheel, and the primary entrance is at the rear), the Mythical logo is to be placed at the top of the plane, over the windows, and with the left edge of the logo near the pilot's windows.

For the right side, the Mythical logo is to be placed at the top of the plane over the windows, and with the underline extending to the pilot's windows.

A-14 DC3

Aircraft—Corporate

In addition to owning an airline, Mythical has its own fleet of corporate aircraft. The planes on the rest of this section are not for commercial use, but are for transporting Mythical executives.

The Mythical logo begins near the nose, and the underline extends to the front door.

O.K.—Here are some planes that might be part of a design program you do someday.

The Mythical logo begins behind the pilot's window with the underline extending toward the aircraft's nose.

Note that corporate aircraft do not use the painted tail. That distinction is reserved for Mythical Airlines.

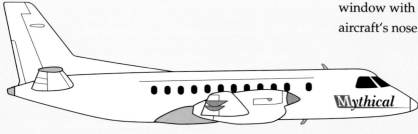

A-24 Saab2000

This small twin engine propeller plane is used by many small businesses. The small size and the large size of windows presents a problem for logo placement. Here, the logo begins at the third passenger window and extends to the edge of the plane.

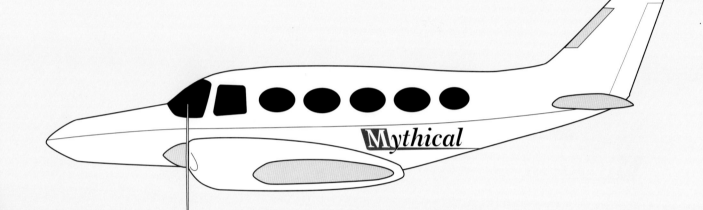

The logo begins at the last passenger window and extends to the wing of the plane.

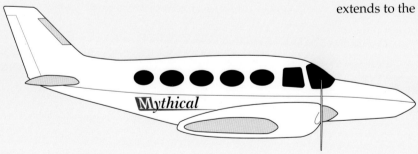

A-41 Cessna414

Aircraft—Corporate

This executive jet has only one logical position for the logo—beginning at the nose, and extending to under the door.

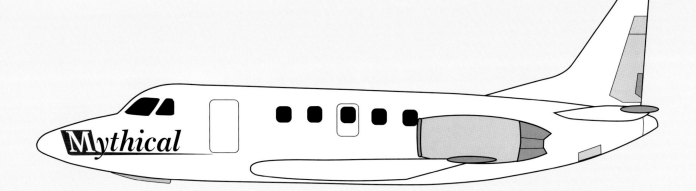

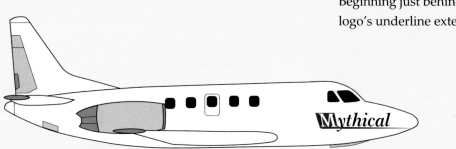

Beginning just behind the pilot's window, the logo's underline extends to the nose's edge.

A-06 jet

The Sabreliner is a popular corporate jet; its compact configuration presents only one logical position for the logo—beginning at the nose and extending to the door.

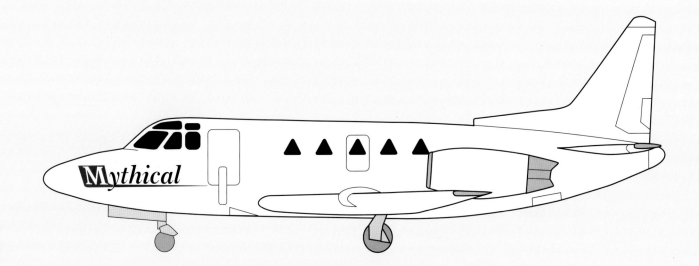

Beginning just behind the pilot's window, the logo's underline extends to the nose's edge.

A-42 Sabreliner65

Aircraft—Corporate

The Jetstream is a popular corporate jet; the Mythical logo is to begin at the nose and extend to behind the engine.

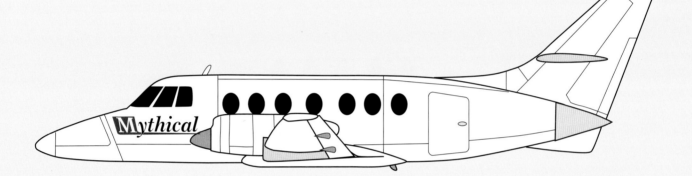

Beginning just behind the pilot's window, the logo's underline extends toward the jet's nose.

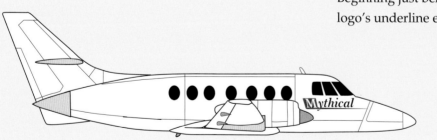

A-22 Jetstream

The Falcon is a popular corporate jet; its compact configuration presents only one logical position for the logo—beginning at the nose and extending to the door.

Note: If the Mythical system did not specify the front of aircraft for the logo, this plane has a nice logo location on the large engine. However, the Mythical system needs consistency. If only one plane were being used, this aircraft might have its logo on the engine — or perhaps the tail.

Beginning just behind the pilot's window, the logo's underline extends toward the jet's nose.

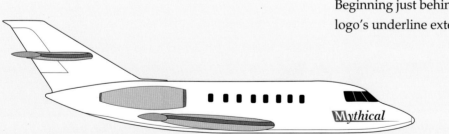

A-10 Falcon20

Aircraft—Corporate

The Mythical corporation has a small fleet of helicopters. The Mythical corporate logo is to be in the position behind the door, and extend to the edge of the body of the craft.

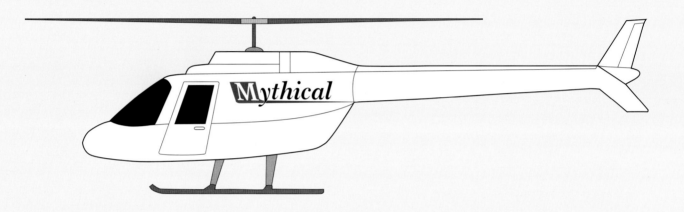

The Mythical corporate logo is to start at the back edge of the helicopter's body with the underline extending to the back edge of the door.

A-18 Heli

Mythical has its own blimp for promotional use. Since the craft is normally seen from the ground as it floats high in the air, the most important factor is to have a logo that is highly visible. Here, the logo is seen at its maximum size.

On both sides of the blimp, the logo is visually centered both horizontally and vertically.

A-19 Blimp

85

Exterior Signage

General signage rules: In most cases, exterior signs will identify specific operating divisions of the Mythical Corporation. Examples are signs for Mythical Car Rental, Mythical Airlines, Mythical Health Club, Mythical Bank, etc.

Modifying Existing Signs: In many cases, existing signs will need to have the information changed to accommodate the new Mythical identity. (The sign structure will remain, since erecting totally new signs can be quite expensive.) When an existing sign is to be modified to include the new Mythical identity, the shape and size of the sign will dictate which logo configuration to use.

In the example shown here, the Mythical logo with division descriptor below is used, and the underline extends to the right edge of the sign. Note that compensating white space must be on the left of the logo.

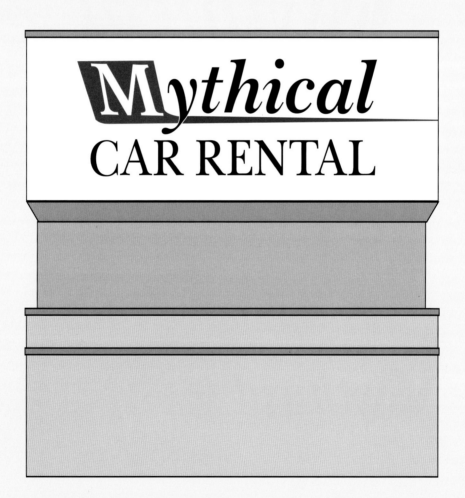

ES-01

In the example shown here, the Mythical logo with division descriptor below is used, and the underline extends to the right edge of the sign. Note that compensating white space must be on the left of the logo. **Caution:** rounded sign areas can present tricky optical illusions involving space relationships. When an existing sign is being modified, there may be no choice but to use this shape. However, when a new sign is being constructed, this style is to be avoided.

Exterior Signage

The use of vertical signs such as this are sometimes the only way to have a new sign approved in municipalities with restrictive ordinances regarding maximum sign size.

The vertical sign can be quite striking, and with proper placement on a property, can be just as effective as a much larger sign.

NOTE: The only approved logo for this type sign is the basic Mythical corporate logo; no logo with additional information (division name, etc.) is permitted.

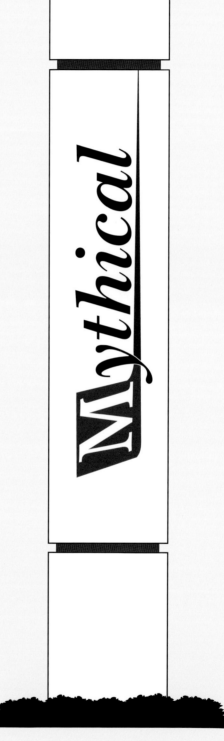

ES-18

This style sign was popular some years ago, but the cost of construction is extremely high when computed on the effective sign size.

This style sign should be used only when it already exists. For new sign construction, a different (more cost effective) style should be chosen.

When dealing with exterior signage, the preferred background for the three-color Mythical Hotels logo is white or a very light color—it is never to be reversed out of black. Mythical Hotel signs should be spotlighted, not lit from behind or from within. Spotlights are to be hidden in foliage below signs.

NOTE: Signs *attached* to the actual hotel building may be in a metallic color, such as gold, bronze, etc.

This style logo does not include an extended underline and should therefore be truly (not just visually) centered.

Mythicalhotel
and**CONVENTION CENTER**

Exterior Signage

Here again, the logo used includes the division name at the right with tails at the bottom.

Note that in this case the underline does not extend to the right of the sign as it is integral in forming the right margin of the logo.

ES-32

Many Mythical facilities will have parking lots that need directional signage. The standard for all such signs is shown on this page. Rules for directional signs are:

1. The standard Mythical logo is to be used. No division name is to be shown, since these are secondary signs. (The reader already knows whether it's Mythical Bank or Mythical Airlines.)

2. For signs pointing left, the underline goes to the edge of the right side.

3. For signs pointing right, the underline goes to the edge of the pointer arrow.

4. For signs pointing forward (not shown here) the style is the same as signs pointing left.

5. The background is always in white, the logo is in the three-color format, and all other type is black.

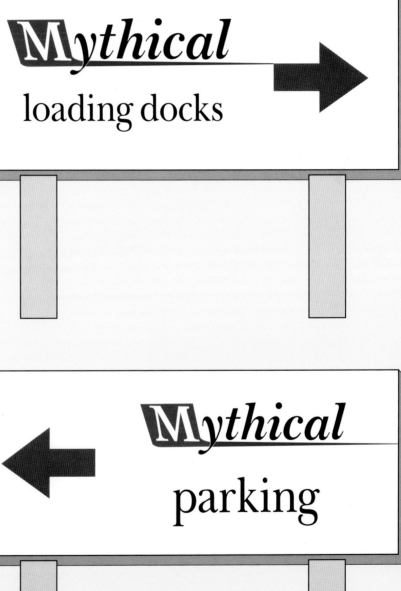

ES-42
ES-43

Exterior Signage

For all signage applications, the Placebo logo is to appear in two colors (black and violet), with the line "a Mythical company" under the logo.

Since the Placebo logo will be used in many countries and a variety of sign layouts, the only general rule is that the logo should have adequate white space on either side, as well as at top and bottom. "Adequate space" may be described as space equal to the width or height of the letter "o" in the Placebo logo.

Pla•cē•bo
a **M**ythical company

Wall plaque style signs feature the Mythical corporate logo, with the descriptor words (such as "executive offices") under the logo set in bold New Baskerville font — all in lower case.

There are two styles of nameplates uses by Mythical. Both styles are shown below.

In either example, the employee name is set is bold New Baskerville, and the Corporate logo with extended underline is used. The employee title is placed in New Baskerville type, all caps, extending to the end of the underline. The logo with employee title is centered under the employee name.

Stephen L. Wilcox
Mythical VICE PRESIDENT

Scott Martin
Mythical EXECUTIVE LEGAL COUNSEL

Interior Signage

Mythical will frequently rent space in office buildings for satellite facilities. This sign should hang from the ceiling outside the primary entrance. It includes the three-color Mythical corporate logo with underline extending to the edge of the sign and compensating white space to the left.

IS-20

Mythical will frequently rent space in office
buildings for satellite facilities. The primary
entrance is to include the Mythical corporate logo.

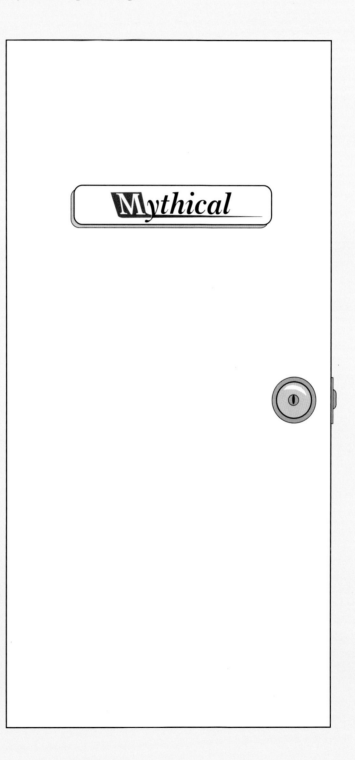

IS-19

Interior Signage

Interior door signage in all Mythical facilities is to include the Mythical corporate logo at the bottom of the visual symbols.

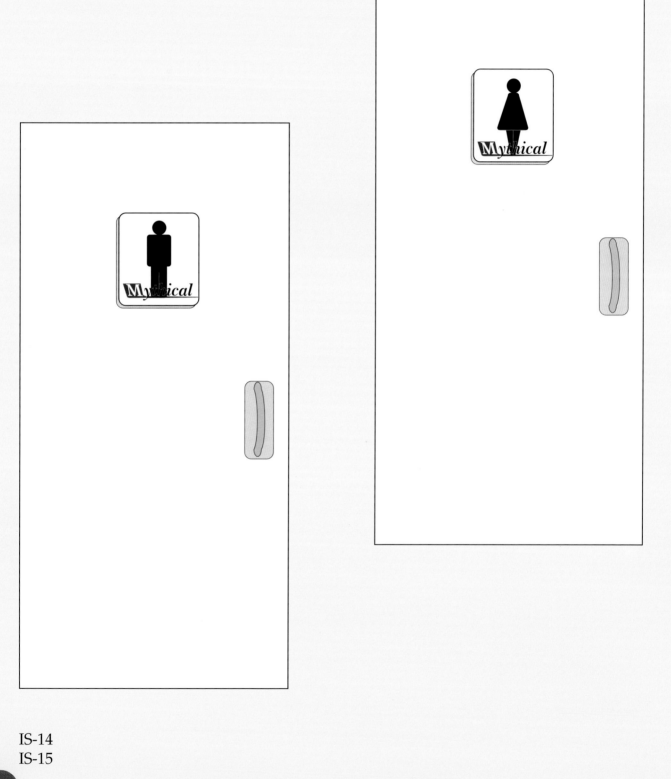

IS-14
IS-15

Interior door signage in all Mythical facilities is to include the Mythical corporate logo at the bottom of the visual symbols.

STAIRS

Mythical

Interior Signage

For specific Mythical divisions, there is often a need to show department information to customers. In these cases, the Mythical logo with division descriptor in three colors is placed at the top.

The department name should be below the logo in New Baskerville font—all lowercase letters.

For specific Mythical divisions, there is often a need to show information to customers at counters, such as airline, bank, car rental, etc. In these cases, the Mythical logo with division descriptor in three colors is placed at the top.

All information below is to be set in Gimlet fonts.

Interior Signage

For specific Mythical divisions, there is often a need to show information to customers at heavy traffic areas, such as lobbies, for divisions such as airline, bank, car rental, etc. In these cases, the

Mythical logo with division descriptor in three colors is placed at the top.

All information below is to be set in Gimlet fonts.

For specific Mythical divisions, there is often a need to show information to customers at heavy traffic areas, such as lobbies, for divisions such as airline, bank, car rental, etc. In these cases, the Mythical logo with division descriptor in three colors is placed at the top.

NOTE: The male figure (template IS-32b) is placed to show a size relationship with the sign. A female figure (IS-32a) is also available on the CD.)

Generally, all information below is to be set in Gimlet fonts. In this case, however, a more elegant feel was wanted to indicate the atmosphere of the event being highlighted. For such an event, Balmoral and Aquitaine Initials font families may be used.

Mythical
CRUISES
dancing and champagne
BALLROOM C
9:00 p.m

IS-32b
IS-03

Interior Signage

For specific division door identification, the Mythical logo with division name underneath is to be used.

Any additional type is to be set in Gimlet fonts.

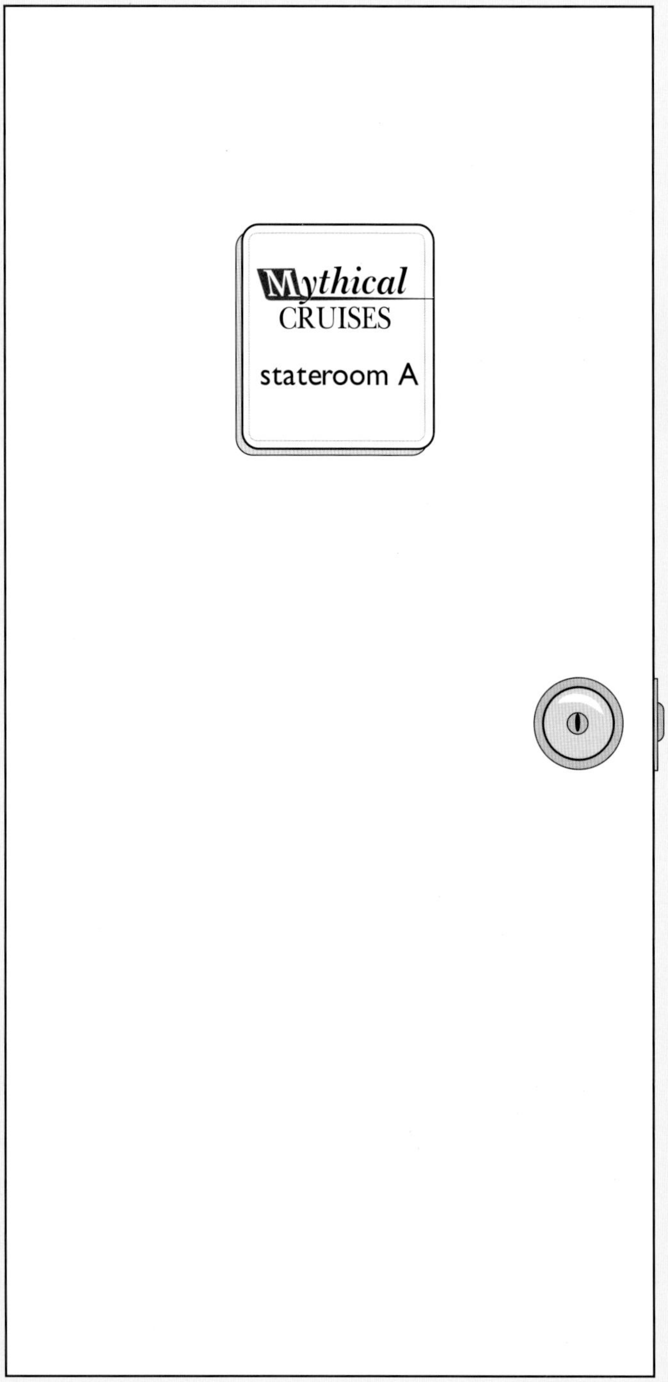

Mythical
CRUISES

stateroom A

For specific Mythical divisions, there is often a need to show information to customers at a desk or counter location. In these cases, the Mythical logo with division descriptor in three colors is placed at the top.

All information is to be set in one of the members of the Gimlet font family.

Interior Signage

This door hanger is for use in Mythical hotels and cruise ships.

Since the primary message is "do not disturb" that is on top and in large type.

The Mythical logo with division name is used. NOTE: Here, the logo is at the bottom of the piece, which is a major departure from the standard of having the logo always on top.

All information is to be set in one of the members of the Gimlet font family.

please
do not
disturb

For specific Mythical divisions, there is often a
need to show information on a large banner.
In these cases, the Mythical logo with division
descriptor in three colors is placed at the top.

All information below is to be in Gimlet fonts.

Interior Signage

Many drug stores and other places which sell Placebo products utilize directional signs such as the ones below. In such cases, the Placebo logo is to be at the top, with the descriptor lines at the bottom in Gimlet fonts.

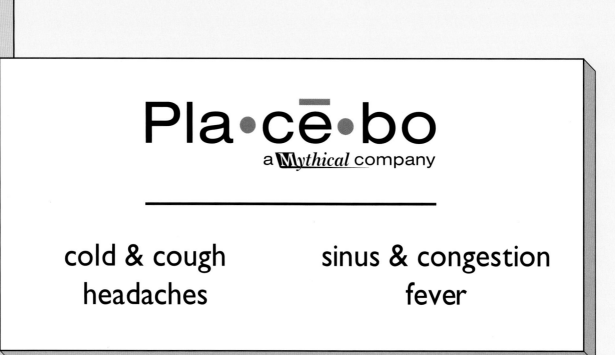

Many drug stores and other places which sell Placebo products utilize freestanding signs such as the one below. In such cases, the Placebo logo is to be at the top. The highlighted event (in this instance "New Items") should be the focal point of the sign. This may be achieved by putting it in bold New Baskerville type and turning approximately 22°. The remaining descriptor lines should be in one of the Gimlet fonts.

NOTE: The female figure (template IS-32a) is placed to show a size relationship with the sign. A male figure (IS-32b) is also available on the CD.)

IS-01
IS-32a

Interior Signage

Many drug stores and other places which sell Placebo products utilize banner-style signs such as the one below. In such cases, the Placebo logo is to be at the top. The highlighted event (in this instance "Special Sale") should be the focal point of the sign. This may be achieved by putting it in bold New Baskerville type and turning approximately 22°. The remaining descriptor lines should be in one of the Gimlet fonts.

IS-28

General rules for Mythical retail graphics:

1. Since a particular product/service is being marketed by a Mythical operating unit, the logo with division descriptor below is always used. The only exception is that the Mythical corporate logo may be used *in addition to* the Mythical logo with division name.

2. The logo is always used in the three-color version.

In the example on this page, the Mythical Car Rental logo appears on each side panel of the retail entrance. The Mythical corporate logo is used above.

Note that the use of *only* the Mythical corporate logo would not be permitted.

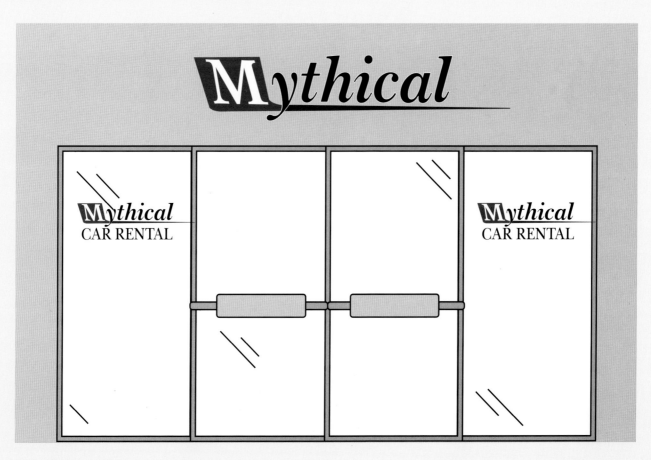

Retail Graphics

In the example on this page, the Mythical Car Rental logo appears on each front panel of the desk. The Mythical corporate logo is used above.

This configuration is desirable here due to the layout of the existing space where logos might appear. Note that the top panel is too narrow to accommodate the Mythical Car Rental logo, while the bottom panel is more suited for its placement there.

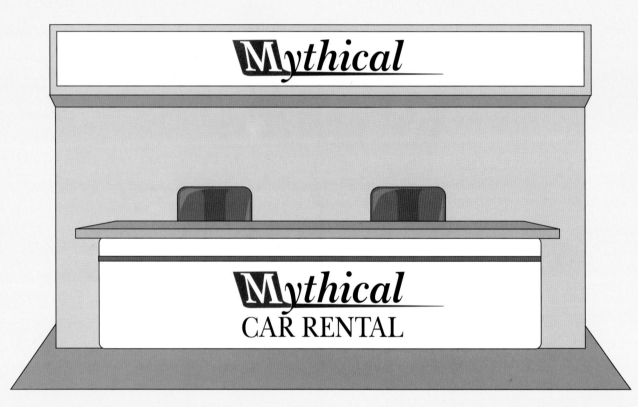

R-08

When only one retail sign is available for a particular venue, it must be the Mythical logo with division descriptor below.

Retail Graphics

This type configuration is typical for trade shows, exhibits, etc. Most standard displays like this have a position at the top for identification, as well as spots on three desks for logos.

In general, the maximum number of logos to be displayed in one location is three—only one may be the Mythical corporate logo; the other two are to be divisional identifiers.

This desk-and-wall layout demonstrates a typical configuration—Mythical corporate logo in the top position (which also has less depth), and the divisional logo at the bottom (which has more depth available).

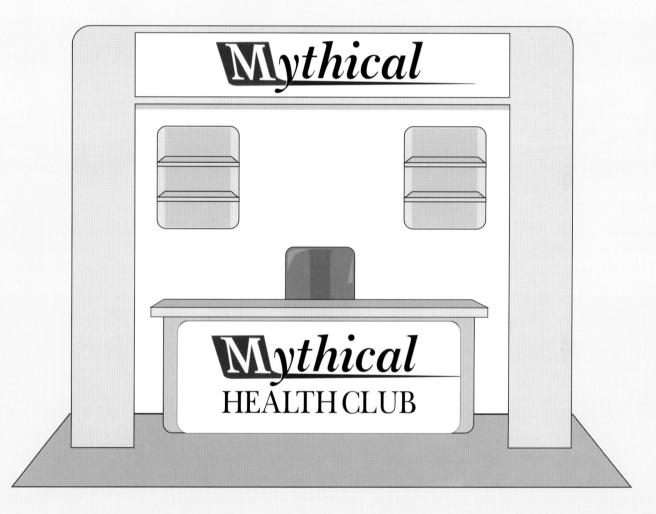

Retail Graphics

When only one elongated space is available for a logo, it is permissible to use the variation of the Mythical logo with division descriptor at right.

Unbreakable rule: when only one position is available for retail identity, use a Mythical logo with division descriptor.

It is not always necessary to use more than one logo, even when space is available. Here, the Mythical Hotel and Convention Center logo at the bottom, where it has five words and takes up two lines. To include another logo at the top (where space is available) would be too much clutter.

Retail Graphics—Placebo

Placebo has a limited number of freestanding locations; most are in developing countries where distribution problems make this necessary. For exteriors, the Placebo logo (with the identifier "a Mythical company" at the bottom) is used. The two-color version—black with violet •-• graphic—is always used.

This is a typical trade show or small space exhibit display. When two locations for a logo are available, they should both be utilized. One should be somewhat larger than the other, in order to create a visual focal point

R-05

Retail Graphics—Placebo

Point of purchase shelves in retail stores are often custom made. Whenever the company controls the design and construction of these shelving systems, the Placebo logo (with Mythical identifier at bottom) should always be at the top of the design—ideally at eye level.

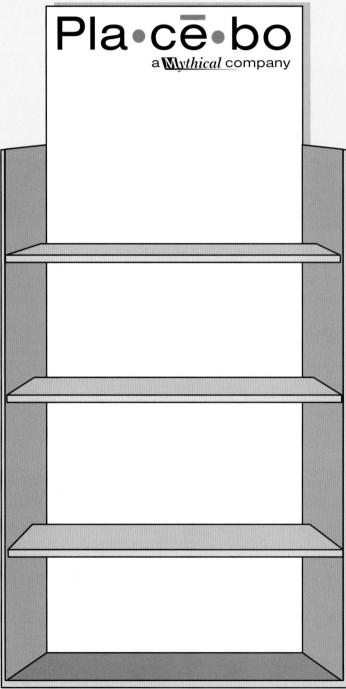

When there is an elongated area for the logo, it is always permissible to use only one side of the allocated space in order to get the full Placebo logo (with "a Mythical company" underneath) on the item.

Packaging—General Rules

Mythical

As this manual is produced, the Mythical Corporation does not market any package goods under the Mythical name. (Placebo packaging is covered elsewhere on this page.) However, the Mythical Hotels division does provide its guests with packaged products such as toothpaste, hand lotion, shampoo, etc. These rules are explained on the next page.

Generic Packages for other Mythical Divisions

While the current Mythical operating units do not have products in packages, there is some limited use of bags, envelopes, etc., such as in the bank and airline division. For these specific uses, the Mythical Corporate logo is to be used. (The customer already knows whether she is in a bank or an airline, so the promotion goal is to highlight the Mythical identity, not a specific division.)

These items are to have a white background, with the three-color logo used.

Placebo Packaging

The Placebo unit is one of the best known prescription and over-the-counter drug companies in the world, and already has hundreds of products on the market.

A long-term project to redesign all Placebo units to include the new Placebo logo (with the identifier "a Mythical company") is now underway. This project is under the direction of the Director of Corporate Identity in the Placebo London office.

Whenever the existing inventory of packages is low, the reorder should include a new package design which adheres to the following rules:

1. The first visual element, at the top of all packages, is the Placebo logo, which includes the identifier ("a Mythical company").

2. The •-• graphic in the Placebo logo may be in any approved color. (See page 11 for color restrictions.) All type elements are to be in black.

3. Due to the need to have designs which stand out on the shelf in a crowded marketplace, the name of the

Many manuals have divider pages for the various sections. (We've left that out of the book due to space requirements.) The divider pages will often have a set of logo use "rules" which are to be followed for that particular section. This page is typical.

product and any associated graphics have no restrictions. However, all new package designs must be approved *in advance of production* by the Director of Corporate Identity for Placebo, located in the London headquarters office.

4. Note that many countries have restrictions on the product information to be included on packages. Before a package is to be produced for any particular country, legal clearance from our in-house counsel must be obtained.

5. The Placebo identity system is designed to allow a wide array of colors for the •-• graphic. In designing product packages, an appropriate color for the particular item should be chosen, such as green for bananas, etc.

Generic Placebo packages

For items such as shopping bags, where no specific product is being identified, the corporate Placebo logo (with "a Mythical company" identifier) should be used. The type should be black, the background should be white, and the •-• graphic should be in a violet color. (Remember that there is no specific color standard for Placebo, since global printing standards vary somewhat, especially in developing countries where Placebo is a major player.)

For any products provided to hotel guests, these design rules are to be followed:

1. The Mythical Hotel and Convention Center logo is to be at the top of the package.

2. An oval shape (vertical or horizontal) is to appear below the logo.

3. The oval will contain the product/package description, in italic Gimlet SSi type, set in all lower case.

4. Any additional copy is to be set below the horizontal oval, in italic New Baskerville Roman type. Vertical ovals may have type set inside.

5. Generic packaging items, such as shopping bags should include only the Mythical Hotel and Convention Center logo.

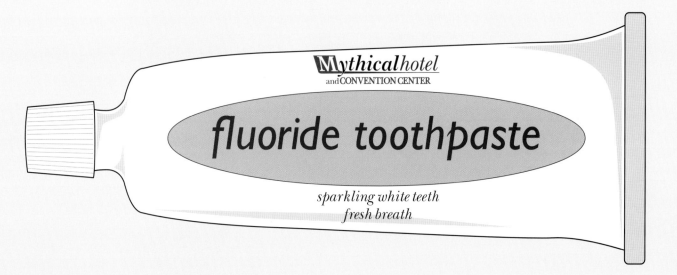

Mythicalhotel
and CONVENTION CENTER

fluoride toothpaste

sparkling white teeth
fresh breath

P-15 tube

Packaging—Hotels

For any products provided to hotel guests, these design rules are to be followed:

1. The Mythical Hotel and Convention Center logo is to be at the top of the package.

2. An oval shape (vertical or horizontal) is to appear below the logo.

3. The oval will contain the product/package description, in italic Gimlet SSi type, set in all lower case.

4. Any additional copy is to be set below the horizontal oval, in italic New Baskerville Roman type. As shown here, vertical ovals may have type set inside.

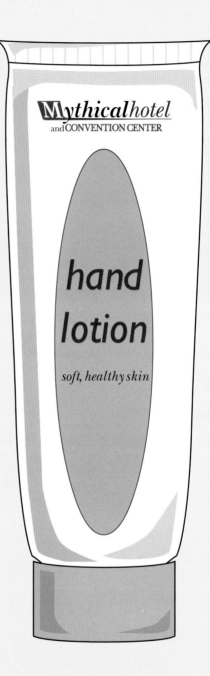

P-16 tube

For any products provided to hotel guests, these design rules are to be followed:

1. The Mythical Hotel and Convention Center logo is to be at the top of the package.

2. An oval shape (vertical or horizontal) is to appear below the logo.

3. The oval will contain the product/package description, in italic Gimlet SSi type, set in all lower case.

4. Any additional copy is to be set below a horizontal oval, in italic New Baskerville Roman type. As shown here, vertical ovals may have type set inside.

P-17 bottle

Packaging—Hotels

Generic hotel packaging items, such as shopping
bags should include only the Mythical Hotel and
Convention Center logo.

P-48 bag

1. The first visual element, at the top of all packages, is the Placebo logo, which includes the identifier ("a Mythical company").

2. The •-• graphic in the Placebo logo may be in any approved color. (See page 11 for color restrictions.) All type elements of the logo are to be in black.

3. The Placebo identity system is designed to allow a strong visual for the product name. Colors should be appropriate for the product.

Packaging—Placebo

Pla•cē•bo
a **M**ythical company

net wt. 8 oz.

organic **banana chips**

no child labor used in any production phase of this item

P-39 box

Packaging—Placebo

1. The first visual element, at the top of all packages, is the Placebo logo, which includes the identifier ("a Mythical company").

2. The •-• graphic in the Placebo logo may be in any approved color. (See page 11 for color restrictions.) All type elements of the logo are to be in black.

3. The Placebo identity system is designed to allow a strong visual for the product name. Colors should be appropriate for the product.

P-41 box

1. The first visual element, at the top of all packages, is the Placebo logo, which includes the identifier ("a Mythical company").

2. The •-• graphic in the Placebo logo may be in any approved color. (See page 11 for color restrictions.) All type elements of the logo are to be in black.

3. The Placebo identity system is designed to allow a strong visual for the product name. Colors should be appropriate for the product.

NOTE: The product name is in one color on a solid stripe background. Since many Placebo products are in highly competitive markets, the design of the package should not be restricted by any graphic limitations.

I have heard many creative people complain about extremely tight restrictions in identity manuals.

"Manuals hinder my creativity," is a common cry.

The good manual will provide structure for visual consistency, while allowing for market-driven creativity.

Pla•cē•bo
a **M**ythical company
gourmet • coffee

Cookie's Cattle Drive
Blend

no bovine were harmed in any production phase of this item

net wt. 8 oz.

P-34 bag

Packaging—Placebo

1. The first visual element, at the top of all packages, is the Placebo logo, which includes the identifier ("a Mythical company").

2. The •-• graphic in the Placebo logo may be in any approved color. (See page 11 for color restrictions.) All type elements of the logo are to be in black.

3. The Placebo identity system is designed to allow a strong visual for the product name. Colors should be appropriate for the product.

NOTE: The product name is placed at an angle, and the Z•h graphic is in a type combination that is not commonly seen on other Placebo packages. Since many Placebo products are in highly competitive markets, the design of the package should not be restricted by any graphic limitations. (Translation: design for sales.)

In a rigid identity system, Placebo dog food could look just like Placebo perfume.

For multi-range products, the identity system must show the Placebo name, but the next important consideration is that the package design must sell products.

P-42 box

1. The first visual element, at the top of all packages, is the Placebo logo, which includes the identifier ("a Mythical company").

2. The •-• graphic in the Placebo logo may be in any approved color. (See page 11 for color restrictions.) All type elements of the logo are to be in black.

3. The Placebo identity system is designed to allow a strong visual for the product name. Colors should be appropriate for the product.

NOTE: There is a graphic below the "pretty for you" hair spray identification. Use of such graphics may be done when the competitive position of the product is enhanced by the addition of a visual identifier. Any graphic that is placed on a package must be within the color restrictions on page 11. Since many Placebo products are in highly competitive markets, the design of the package should not be restricted by any graphic limitations. (Translation: design for sales.)

The addition of this graphic enhances the visual quality of this package.

Many manuals would prohibit the use of such visuals.

The people who create graphic standards should remember that the ultimate goal of the firm is profit.

Pla•cē•bo
a Mythical company

pretty•for•you
hair spray

10 oz.

Packaging—Placebo

1. The first visual element, at the top of all packages, is the Placebo logo, which includes the identifier ("a Mythical company").

2. The •-• graphic in the Placebo logo may be in any approved color. (See page 11 for color restrictions.) All type elements of the logo are to be in black.

3. The Placebo identity system is designed to allow a strong visual for the product name. Colors should be appropriate for the product.

When a manual gives some degree of autonomy to design decisions, how does a company assure quality design?

Many large firms have a director of corporate identity, whose office must approve <u>all</u> items not covered specifically in the manual.

Pla•cē•bo
a **M**ythical company

DEAD BUGS

poison · for · pests

many, many insects were harmed in the production of this item

net wt. 16 oz.

pack*1

1. The first visual element, at the top of all packages, is the Placebo logo, which includes the identifier ("a Mythical company").

2. The •-• graphic in the Placebo logo may be in any approved color. (See page 11 for color restrictions.) All type elements of the logo are to be in black.

3. The Placebo identity system is designed to allow a strong visual for the product name. Colors should be appropriate for the product.

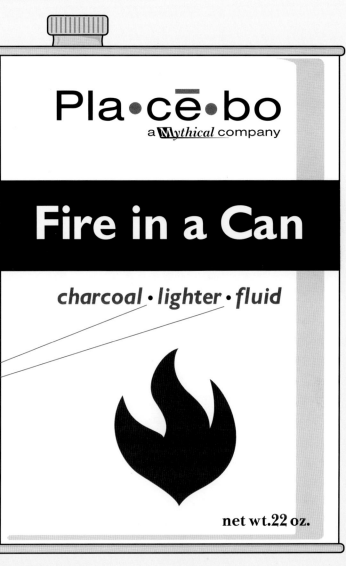

This is a small design touch — note that the dividers between words on many Placebo packages are . elements, very similar to the •-• graphic in the logo.

This is not a written rule in the original manual, but a nice touch that evolved. It would likely become a topic of the next manual revision.

Packaging—Placebo

Many package presentations must be made by showing all six sides of a box. This template is designed to show the flat printed piece which will become a container.

There are other shapes of this style template on the CD-ROM which accompanies this book. They are found on page 171.

Pla•ce•bo
a **M**ythical company

Intern•ahh

cures
yeast infection
overnight

2.5 oz

Pla•ce•bo
a **M**ythical company

Pla•ce•bo
a **M**ythical company

Intern•ahh

cures
yeast infection
overnight

2.5 oz

Pla•ce•bo
a **M**ythical company

Active Ingredient:
97% megazoid who-knows-what.

Inert Ingredients:
petroleum jelly, cornstarch, water, strawberries, mustard plaster, cod liver oil, polysorbate 80, meat by-products, & vitamin B12.

P-45 box

For items such as shopping bags, where no specific product is being identified, the corporate Placebo logo (with "a Mythical company" identifier) should be used. The type should be black, the background should be white, and the •-• graphic should be in a violet color. (Remember that there is no specific color standard for Placebo, since global printing standards vary somewhat, especially in developing countries where Placebo is a major player.)

P-47 bag

Promotional Items

For most promotional items, the goal is to promote the Mythical Corporation, not a specific operating division.

When the space available for a logo allows, the Mythical logo underline should extend to the right of the item. NOTE: Do not try to fill a large space with the logo. The objective is "quiet" communication, not a "loud" message. Note how the logo on the clock takes up only a portion of the space available; it looks much better than if the logo were to extend all the way across the bottom of the clock.

Use of Mythical logo with division name: In limited instances, the Mythical logo with the division name will appear. This is normally done when the promotional item is connected to an event at a Mythical division location, or the item is given to primary customers of a particular division, such as frequent flyers of Mythical Airlines.

PR-20 clock

Here, the space available for a logo is very large. In cases such as this, no attempt should be made to have the underline extend to the right edge. Rather, the design is much cleaner when the logo is centered. In addition, there is no logical place to put the logo so that it could have the underline extend to the edge.

PR-43 case

Promotional Items

Here, there is a large amount of space available for a logo. It could be properly placed in the center of the cover, but in this case it appears at the bottom, with the logo underline extending to the edge of the page. This is another example of the "quiet" use of the logo, where the design is not using the maximum space available.

PR-42 padfolio

Here, there is a large amount of space available for a logo. It could be properly placed in the lower right corner, with the underline extending to the edge, but in this case it appears centered. This is another example of the "quiet" use of the logo, where the design is not using the maximum space available.

PR-53 flashlight

Note this logo spec, compared with that on the previous page. In both examples, the logo could be placed in several different sizes and positions. It would be difficult to write a set of "rules" to cover these two items. The lesson is that ID manuals should not be overly restrictive, with rules that are too contrived.

Promotional Items

The Mythical logo could be placed at right, or it could be centered. Here, the designer has chosen to place in the middle.

This example shows that many items have more than one possible location for a the logo placement.

The well-planned corporate identity manual will assure some degree of consistency of the logo system, but will NOT take away all creative decisions from individuals..

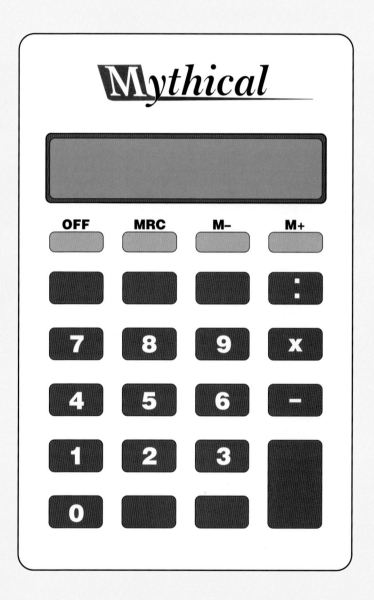

PR-24 calculator

For extremely elongated items, the Mythical logo needs to be placed in a size and configuration that simultaneously (a) has a tasteful "quiet" appearance, and (b) still communicates.

PR-54 ruler
PR-06 pen

Promotional Items

This clock includes the Mythical logo with the division descriptor at right.

In this example, the Mythical Airlines logo is used, since this promotion was specifically directed to the frequent flyers of that division.

A well-written manual will give specifications which can be applied to other items which are not even shown. Note the instructions at left — on promoting a particular Mythical division — are also a standard for items other than clocks.

PR-22 clock

The paper napkins for special events at the Mythical Hotel and Convention Center include the divisional name, since it is for on-site use.

Note the instructions at left regarding use of the logo for on-site consumption. The same rule could be applied to items such as drinking glasses at the hotel, or airsick bags on aircraft. Since every item cannot be shown, the manual can be consulted for a similar use rule which applies in a particular instance.

PR-01 napkin

Promotional Items

These mugs include the Mythical Hotels' logo
with division descriptor at right and details below
since they are to be given to attendees of a confer-
ence at the hotel.

PR-32 mug

The golf ball has the Mythical corporate logo (no division name) since it is an item given to customers/prospects of any and all Mythical operating units.

The golf tee includes the Mythical Hotel logo, since it is used on the premises by Mythical guests at the Mythical golf course.

PR-49 golfball
PR-50 tee

Promotional Items

The Mythical Health Club logo is used in this instance, since it is a promotional item meant specifically for members of the club.

Note that it's used in a size to "quietly" speak the Mythical name.

PR-62 cooler

Promotional Items

The squeeze bottle for Mythical Health Club customers uses the Mythical logo with division name at the bottom. Note that the underline extends to a place where it is optically at the right edge of a curved surface.

PR-39 squeeze

Promotional Items

On the key ring at the top, the Mythical Hotel logo is used, since it is for on-premises use of customers.

Below, the Placebo logo is shown in its only approved configuration for promotional use: 2-color Placebo logo, with "a Mythical company" underneath.

PR-15 keyring
PR-10 keyring

Mythical Corporation ties may be worn by employees—with or without a uniform. This design was carefully chosen because it is equally appropriate for wear with a suit, with a blazer and khakis, or simply with a white shirt and no jacket.

Note the only approved striping configuration for Mythical ties:

> Wide Blue
> Wide White
> Narrow Blue
> Narrow White
> Narrow Red
> Wide White
>
> Repeat the pattern

Note: Scarves with this same color and striping configuration are available for female employees.

Many companies produce ties which include the company logo. For Mythical, this is not a good option, especially since the Placebo division would require its own design. This classic stripe is similar to the school ties which are popular in England.

C-33 tie

Clothing

This blazer is normally navy blue, but it is shown white in order to demonstrate clearly the position and colors of the logo.

For use on blazers, the Mythical logo is in its standard three-color configuration. However, since a medium blue is one of the colors, it will not show up well on a solid navy blue background. In order to overcome this limitation, the entire logo is

to have a white outline around the outside of all the type and design elements. (See inset at bottom of page.)

Note that the end of the underline extends to the right side of the pocket. The left side of the pocket has an equal amount of compensating white space (actually, navy blue space) in order to center the type on the pocket.

C-32 blazer

The Mythical logo may appear on several types of long-sleeve shirts such as white dress shirts, light blue dress shirts, or blue work shirts.

In each case, the embroidered logo is in three colors; the underline extends to the right edge of the pocket. Compensating white space is on the left in order to center the type on the pocket.

Mythical

C-24 shirt

Clothing

The Mythical logo may appear on several types of long-sleeve shirts such as white dress shirts, light blue dress shirts, or blue work shirts.

In each case, the embroidered logo is in three colors; the underline extends to the right edge of the pocket. Compensating white space is on the left in order to center the type on the pocket.

NOTE: The short-sleeved Mythical shirt is never to be worn with a jacket and tie, as short-sleeved shirts are not considered to be dress attire.

C-22 shirt

Sweatshirts are distributed for promotional use to customers, as well as being items which may be purchased (at cost) by employees. In order to present a quality image, the Mythical corporate logo is always embroidered—never printed or silk screened.

The logo is to be sized so that it is no larger than would appear on a dress shirt pocket.

C-05 tshirt

Clothing

The jacket shown here is of 100% wool, with leather sleeves and collar. It is presented to Mythical employees who meet certain incentives, and it is considered to be a prestigious award.

The Mythical corporate logo is shown here embroidered in three colors. It is sized to be approximately 60% of the total width of the left side jacket panel.

C-28a jacket

Many Mythical employees take part in summer softball and baseball leagues; it is our policy to sponsor teams whenever an employee requests it.

In addition, Mythical sponsors a number of youth league teams all over the nation.

Standard uniform design is for the Mythical corporate logo to be on the left breast, embroidered in three colors.

It would be possible to have the logo much larger, but we choose in these cases to have it in a size that is understated.

Mythical

C-14 jersey

Clothing

Many Mythical employees take part in basketball leagues; it is our policy to sponsor teams whenever an employee requests it.

In addition, Mythical sponsors a number of youth league teams all over the nation.

Standard uniform design is for the Mythical corporate logo to be on the left breast, embroidered in three colors.

It would be possible to have the logo much larger, but we choose in these cases to have it in a size that is understated.

C-11 tank

Clothing

Many Mythical employees take part in basketball leagues; it is our policy to sponsor teams whenever an employee requests it.

In addition, Mythical sponsors a number of youth league teams all over the nation.

Standard uniform design is for the Mythical corporate logo to be on the left pants leg, embroidered in three colors.

It would possible to have the logo much larger, but we choose in these cases to have it in a size that is understated.

C-12 shorts

I have seen manuals that were so rigidly restrictive that this logo would be specified to "always be 3.5 inches across." Rules like this don't consider the fact that shorts for a child are much smaller than those for an adult (and the logo would be far larger on a proportional basis).

Clothing

Baseball-style caps are very popular for use as promotions, for customers, and for employees who take part in sports leagues where we sponsor teams. The Mythical corporate logo is to appear in two places on baseball style caps: the standard front position, as well as on the back. On the front, the logo is to take up no more than 70% of the center panel(s). On the back, it is to be no wider than the opening.

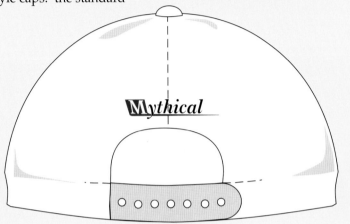

C-34 hat

This hooded jacket is designed for Mythical employees who are outside in cold weather conditions.

The Mythical logo is to be embroidered in three colors and is to take up approximately 50% of the width of the left jacket panel.

C-26 jacket

Clothing

This toboggan-type cap is designed for Mythical employees who are outside in cold weather conditions.

The Mythical logo is to be embroidered in three colors and is to take up approximately 25% of the cap when it is laying flat.

C-35 toboggan

Many Mythical employees work in areas where head protection is needed. The standard hard hat is white, with the Mythical corporate logo centered on the front of the item. The logo is to take up approximately 40% of the hat as seen from the front.

NOTE: Divisional logos are never used on hard hats, as the location makes it clear which company is involved. The goal here is to promote the link with the overall Mythical corporate identity, not a specific division.

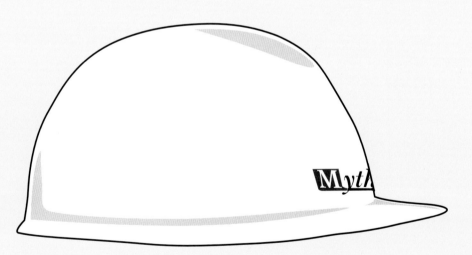

C-37 hardhat

Clothing

Polo style knit shirts are very popular as promotional items, gifts to customers and prospects, and are available for purchase (at cost) by employees.

A variety of colors are available. All polo style shirts are to have the Mythical corporate logo embroidered in three colors. The logo is to take up no more than 30% of the space between the buttons and the sleeve seam.

C-16 polo

Coveralls are worn by a variety of maintenance and technical people—in occupations as diverse as aircraft mechanic, lab technician, etc. In all cases the coverall is to include the Mythical corporate logo, embroidered in three colors. The underline is to extend to the right edge of the pocket; compensating white space is to be at left.

NOTE: The divisional logos are never used on coveralls; the location makes it quite obvious which operating unit is represented.

IMPORTANT: Each year, Mythical will sponsor an "Elvis Impersonator" contest, in which employees who participate will be given a "jumpsuit" with Mythical logo in 3 colors, adorned with hundreds of colored rhinestones. Finalists will be given a silk scarf, with standard Mythical color striping system as shown on page 147.

The overall winner will be given a one-year leave of absence to go on tour.

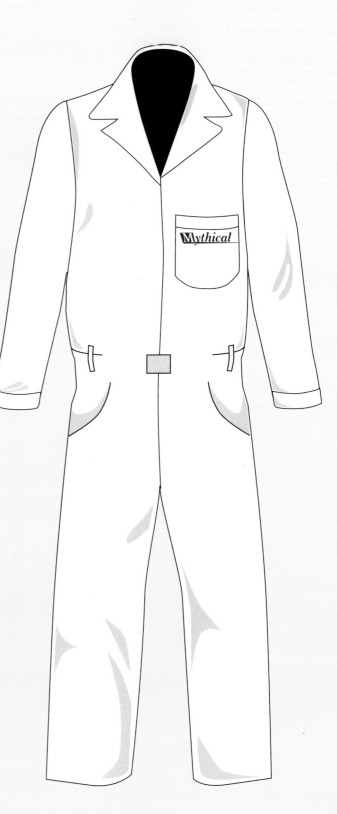

Sorry.

I got a little carried away.

DC

C-29 coveralls

Clothing

Lightweight jackets are very popular as promotional items, gifts to customers and prospects, and are available for purchase (at cost) by employees.

A variety of colors are available. All lightweight jackets are to have the Mythical corporate logo embroidered in three colors. It is to take up no more than 50% of the width of the left jacket panel.

C-27 jacket

The Mythical hotels provide bathrobes in all guest rooms. The terry cloth robes are to always be in white, with the three-color Corporate logo embroidered.

NOTE: the hotel division logo is not used here, even though the general rules (use the divisional logo when items are used on premises) would indicate otherwise.

The embroidery into terry cloth is very complex, and to include the hotel identifier would create a logo that is either too large, or too busy.

Mythical

C-31 robe

Clothing—Placebo

Placebo has few promotional items. For many years, Placebo has given free product samples to people in a position to recommend their use to customers.

In the few cases where promotional clothing is to be used, it will be a quality t-shirt, with the Placebo logo in black and violet. The logo is to be on the left breast, and the logo is to take up no more than 45% of the width of the chest of the shirt.

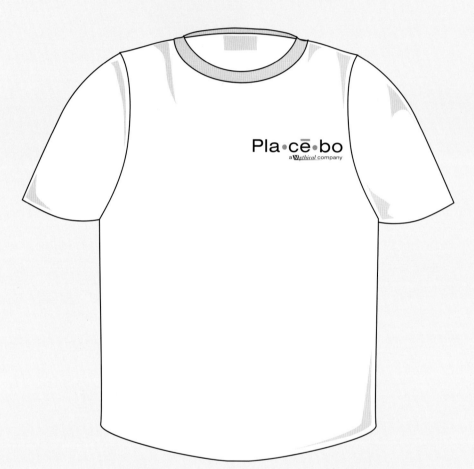

C-01 tshirt

Placebo employees in many parts of the world wear lab coats in their daily routine. For all these lab coats, the Placebo (with "a Mythical company" underneath) is to be either printed, silk screened, or embroidered onto the pocket. The two-color version (black and violet) is to be used.

Pla•ce•bo
a Mythical company

C-30 labcoat

Personal Identification—Mythical

Since the primary purpose of identification cards is security, each division name is to be used with the Mythical logo.

All ID cards are to have the following standards:

1. The Mythical logo with division name is to be at the top of the card, in the three-color format. The underline is to extend to the right edge of the card; the compensating white space is at the left. The employee's name is to be in a Gimlet font.

2. Each division is to have a different background color for personnel photographs.

> Corporate employees = light blue
> Mythical airlines = red
> Mythical hotels = green
> Mythical bank and trust = gray
> Mythical car rental = orange
> Mythical transport = brown
> Mythical health club = purple

As a new division becomes part of the Mythical corporation, the appropriate color will be added to this list.

Position of the Mythical ID badge: As an additional security precaution, all Mythical ID badges are to be worn on the *right* side of the shirt or jacket, not the left. Anyone wearing a Mythical ID badge on the left will be considered a potential security problem.

Mythical CAR RENTAL Clarke Smathers

This is one reason why identity manuals are produced in ring binders. Changes may happen frequently, and it is relatively easy and cost effective to change only a few pages in a manual.

Another note on manual changes: there are two easy ways to have page numbering systems that allow easy changes. When a page is being replaced by two new pages, use either (1) page 10 and 10a, OR (2) use section page numbers, such as A-22, A-23, etc. (Using this may mean you have to replace an entire section.)

Personal Identification—Placebo

All Placebo ID cards are to have the following standards:

1. The Placebo logo is to be at the top of the card, in the two-color format; the line "a Mythical company" is to be under the Placebo logo. The employee's name is to be in a Gimlet font.

2. Each Placebo location is to use the same background color for ID photographs. This cloth or paper background standard is to be established, and the personnel department of each operation is to have this photo location in a single, secure location within the facility.

Position of the Placebo ID badge: As an additional security precaution, all Placebo ID badges are to be worn on the *right* side of the shirt or jacket, not the left. Anyone wearing a Placebo ID badge on the left will be considered a potential security problem.

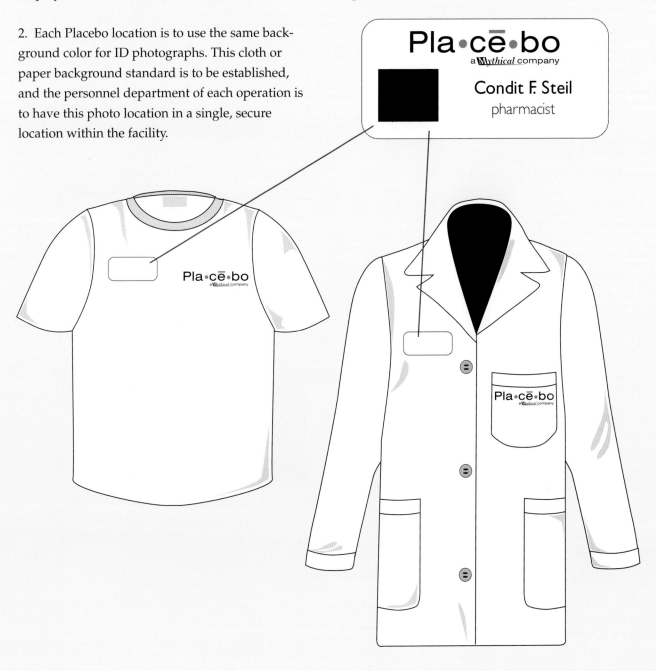

Pla•cē•bo
a Mythical company
Condit F. Steil
pharmacist

Advertising Standards—Mythical

Advertising standards are not intended to restrict the creativity of people who produce ads for the various Mythical companies. The purpose is to assure that the logo is used properly, and to get maximum impact for the Mythical name and logo.

Rules for Mythical advertising:

1. When the ad is for a particular division, the Mythical logo with division descriptor below is to be used. In divisional ads, a particular product or service is being advertised. It is important that the logo reflect this.

2. When a corporate ad is run (not featuring a single division) the Mythical logo is to be used.

3. Whenever possible, the three-color logo is to be used. The only exception to this is when the ad is otherwise in black and white.

4. The logo is to be in one of two positions, as illustrated on the samples on this page.

(a) Logo in lower right corner. Divide the page into eight equal rectangles; the logo is to fit into the lower right corner.

(b) Divide the ad into seven equal horizontal segments; the logo is to be placed in the bottom segment.

There are no other approved positions for the logo. This is most important, as research has shown that the greatest impact of an advertisement is made when the logo is in one of these positions. **There are to be no exceptions to this rule.**

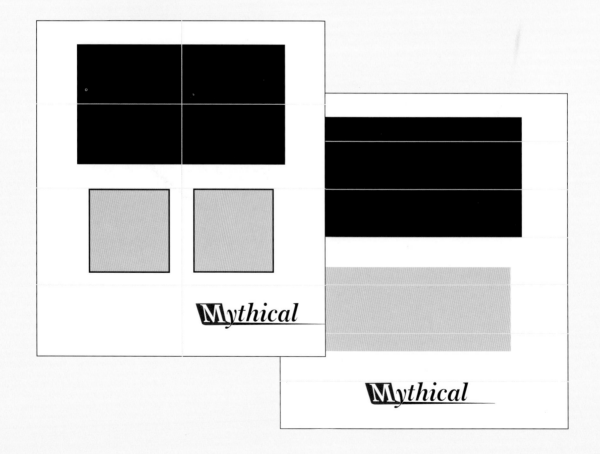

Advertising Standards—Placebo

Advertising standards are not intended to restrict the creativity of people who produce ads for the various Placebo units around the world. The purpose is to assure that the logo is used properly, and to get maximum impact for the Placebo name and logo.

Rules for Placebo advertising:

1. The Placebo logo is always to include the line "a Mythical company." There are no exceptions to this rule.

2. Whenever possible, the two-color Placebo logo (black and violet) is to be used. The only exception to this is when the ad is otherwise in black and white.

3. The logo is to be in one of two positions, as illustrated on the samples on this page.

(a) Logo in lower right corner. Divide the page into eight equal rectangles; the logo is to fit into the lower right corner.

(b) Divide the ad into seven equal horizontal segments; the logo is to be placed in the bottom segment.

There are no other approved positions for the logo. This is most important, as research has shown that the greatest impact of an advertisement is made when the logo is in one of these positions. **There are to be no exceptions to this rule.**

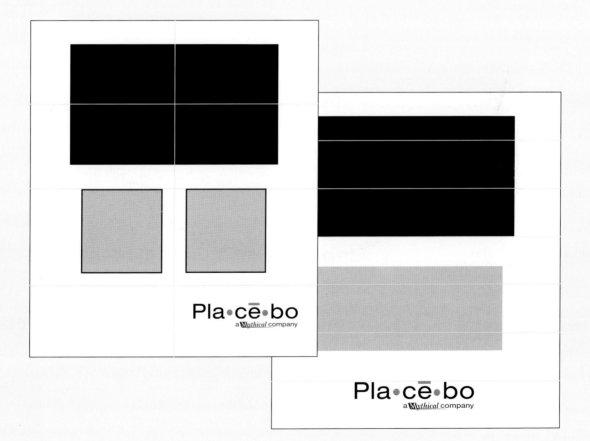

Additional templates on the CD-ROM

All the templates (trucks, clothing, etc.) found in this book are included on the CD-ROM which accompanies this publication.

In addition to the large number of templates shown in the "Mythical Corporate Identity Manual," there are more than 200 more templates included on the CD-ROM. The remaining templates are shown on the following 3 pages, along with the name under which they may be found on the CD.

Using the CD-ROM templates with Macintosh: the templates are in standard EPS format. They may be "placed" in a page layout or drawing program, or opened in a drawing program such as Macromedia FreeHand or Adobe Illustrator.

Using the CD-ROM templates with PC computers: the templates are in DOS EPS format. They may be "placed" in a page layout or drawing program. Some drawing programs may open the templates.

A-01 B707	A-02 DC8-50	A-03 DC8-60	A-04 B747-100	A-7 DHC6	A-11 DC9-10	A-12 DC9-80	A-13 DC9
A-17 Fokker614	A-20 Heli J-Bird	A-21 DHC8	A-23 Fmetro	A-25 GulfstreamIV	A-27 Challenger	A-34 Airbus330	A-35 Airbus300
A-36 Airbus340	A-37 Lear	A-38 Pnavajo	A-39 Pchieftain	A-40 Cessna404	C-02 tshirt	C-03 tshirt	C-04 tshirt
C-06 tshirt	C-07 tshirt	C-08 henley	C-09 tneck	C-10 sweatshirt	C-13 jersey	C-15 jersey	C-17 polo
C-18 polo	C-19 polo	C-20 polo	C-21 shirt	C-23 shirt	C-25 jacket	C-28b jacket	C-36 hardhat
C-38 helmet	E-02	E-03	E-04	E-05	E-06	E-07	E-08
E-09	E-10	E-11	E-12	E-14	E-15	E-16	A=Airlines C=Clothing E=ExtSign

E-17	E-19	E-20	E-21	E-22	E-23	E-24	E-25
E-27	E-28	E-29	E-30	E -31	E-33	E-35	E-36
E-37	E-38 PARKING	E- 39	E- 40	E-41	E-44 PARKING	E-45 NO PARKING	E-46 DO NOT ENTER
E-47 PARKING	E-48	E-49	IS-02	IS-09 EXIT	IS-10 RESTROOMS	IS-11 RESTROOMS	IS-12
IS-13	IS-16	IS-21	IS-22	IS-25	IS-29	IS-30	IS-31
P-01diskette	P-02 tape	P-03 tapecase	P-04 CD	P-05 CD case	P-06 spiralbound	P-07 jar	P-08 jar
P-09 jar	P-10 jar	P-11 bottle	P-12 bottle	P-13 jar	P-14 bottle	P-18 bottle	P-19 bottle
P-20 bottle	P-21 bottle	P-22 bottle	P-23 bottle	P-24 bottle	P-25 bottle	P-26 bottle	P-27 bottle
P-28 bottle	P-29 can	P-30 container	P-31 container	P-32 bag	P-33 bag	P-35 box	P-36 box
E=ExtSign IS=Int Signs P=Packaging PR=Promo	P-37 box	P-38 box	P-40 box	P-43 box	P-44 box	P-46 box	PR-02 matches

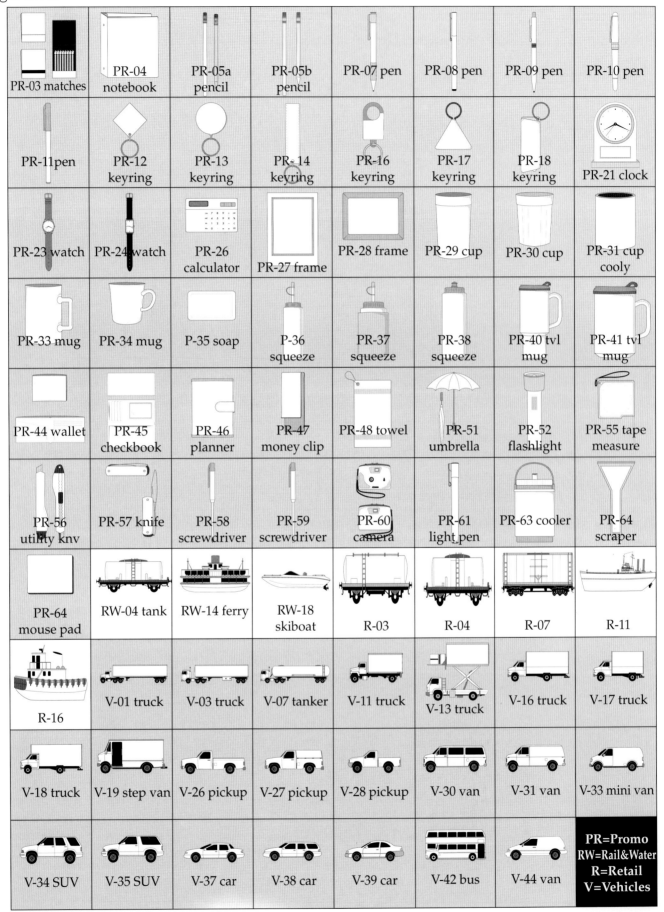

LogoPower

PR-03 matches	PR-04 notebook	PR-05a pencil	PR-05b pencil	PR-07 pen	PR-08 pen	PR-09 pen	PR-10 pen
PR-11 pen	PR-12 keyring	PR-13 keyring	PR-14 keyring	PR-16 keyring	PR-17 keyring	PR-18 keyring	PR-21 clock
PR-23 watch	PR-24 watch	PR-26 calculator	PR-27 frame	PR-28 frame	PR-29 cup	PR-30 cup	PR-31 cup cooly
PR-33 mug	PR-34 mug	P-35 soap	P-36 squeeze	PR-37 squeeze	PR-38 squeeze	PR-40 tvl mug	PR-41 tvl mug
PR-44 wallet	PR-45 checkbook	PR-46 planner	PR-47 money clip	PR-48 towel	PR-51 umbrella	PR-52 flashlight	PR-55 tape measure
PR-56 utility knv	PR-57 knife	PR-58 screwdriver	PR-59 screwdriver	PR-60 camera	PR-61 light pen	PR-63 cooler	PR-64 scraper
PR-64 mouse pad	RW-04 tank	RW-14 ferry	RW-18 skiboat	R-03	R-04	R-07	R-11
R-16	V-01 truck	V-03 truck	V-07 tanker	V-11 truck	V-13 truck	V-16 truck	V-17 truck
V-18 truck	V-19 step van	V-26 pickup	V-27 pickup	V-28 pickup	V-30 van	V-31 van	V-33 mini van
V-34 SUV	V-35 SUV	V-37 car	V-38 car	V-39 car	V-42 bus	V-44 van	**PR=Promo RW=Rail&Water R=Retail V=Vehicles**

172